THE
CLASSICAL
COMPENDIUM

PHILIP MATYSZAK

THE CLASSICAL COMPENDIUM

with 109 illustrations

Thames & Hudson

For my brother, Conrad

Half-title *Roman musical duo, featuring Hydralus and Cornu (water organ and horn). The image is from a mosaic found in Nennig, Germany, and shows the pair entertaining at the gladiatorial games.*

Frontispiece *Oedipus solving the riddle of the Sphinx on an Athenian-style drinking cup from Volci, Italy.*

First published in 2009 in hardcover in the United States of America by Thames & Hudson Inc., 500 Fifth Avenue, New York, New York 10110

thamesandhudsonusa.com

Library of Congress Catalog Card Number 2009901946

ISBN 978-0-500-05162-7

Printed and bound in China by SNP Leefung Printers Ltd

CONTENTS

INTRODUCTION

The ancients were great compilers of works of miscellanea in their own right, and compiling this book has required the skills of an editor – in the true Roman sense of the word – as much as those of an author. The basis for selection was that each story should above all be interesting and entertaining, but that it should also tell us something about the way the Greeks and Romans viewed the world, and how their perceptions and preoccupations were sometimes remarkably similar to ours today. Where the story being told is evidently untrue, or at least stretches one's credulity, I've pointed this out. Many of the things in this book even the Greeks and Romans considered quirky or bizarre, whereas other facts are included because, while they are extraordinary today, the people of the time thought nothing of them.

The libraries of Pliny and Plutarch take us to a different classical world from that of austere temples and abstruse grammar. Here we meet people who like nothing more than a good yarn, and then to recycle that yarn at dinner parties. And indeed, many of the tales found in this book were originally collected over the winecups as diners swapped anecdotes after a sumptuous meal in the *triclinium*. Nothing, one suspects, would delight those raconteurs more than the knowledge that some of their stories are still in circulation today, 2,000 years later, as fresh and entertaining as when they were first told.

I

INCREDIBLE
JOURNEYS
WONDERS

In the ancient world, people tended to stay where they were put. Travel was difficult and expensive, not to mention dangerous. Nevertheless, despite the hazards and difficulties, some people travelled far. These wanderers came home with stories of faraway peoples and wonderful sights, some real, others spun from purest fantasy.

Alexandrian coin depicting the
Great Lighthouse on Pharos.

THE MARCH OF THE TEN THOUSAND

After a series of wars with the Persians during the fifth century BC, it became clear that the Greeks were generally superior soldiers. Consequently Cyrus, a member of the Persian royal family, collected over 10,000 Greek hoplites to overthrow his brother, Artaxerxes II, the Persian King of Kings. The rebel army met the king's forces at Cunaxa, on the Euphrates, just north of Babylon.

The Greeks did well in the battle, unlike other parts of Cyrus' army; Cyrus himself was slain. However, the Persians destroyed the Greeks' camp and supplies, and when the Greek commanders attempted to negotiate, they were treacherously seized and executed – leaving 10,000 soldiers in the middle of a hostile empire with no supplies, base, employer or leaders.

The Greeks elected new leaders, and began the slow process of marching 500 miles (800 km) back through the Persian empire to safety. The Persians continued to attack them until the Greeks formed groups of slingshots and cavalry with which to fight back. From Mesopotamia, the army moved to Kurdistan, and then into Armenia, suffering steady attrition along the way from blizzards, lack of supplies, frostbite and skirmishes with the enemy. Eventually the army was reduced to some 6,000 men. Xenophon, one of the leaders of the army, wrote a personal account of the journey called the *Anabasis*, commonly known today as 'The March of the 10,000'.

Perhaps the most dramatic moment of the book is when Xenophon became aware of a disturbance at the head of the column. Suspecting another attack he hurried forward to hear shouts of 'Thalatta! Thalatta!' (The sea! The sea!). Though much marching and fighting remained to be done, the Greeks had brought themselves to safety.

PHOENICIANS IN CAPE TOWN?

Herodotus amassed many travellers' tales, some more credible than others. The following story tells of an amazing feat – the circumnavigation of Africa in 600 BC.

The Egyptian king Necho ... sent out a fleet manned by a Phoenician crew with orders to sail [south and] west and return to Egypt and the Mediterranean by way of the Pillars of Hercules [i.e. go anti-clockwise around Africa, returning via the Straits of Gibraltar]. The Phoenicians sailed from the Arabian Gulf into the southern ocean, and every autumn put in at some convenient spot on the coast, sowed a patch of ground, and waited for next year's harvest. Then, having got in their grain, they put to sea again, and after two full years at sea rounded the Pillars of Hercules in the course of the third year, and returned to Egypt. These men made a statement which I do not myself believe, though others may, to the effect that as they sailed west around the southern end of Africa, they had the sun on their right – to the north. HERODOTUS, *THE HISTORIES*, 4.42

If this story is correct (and their sighting of the sun to the north would suggest that the voyagers did at least cross the equator), then Africa was first circumnavigated some 2,000 years before Vasco da Gama managed it.

HOW TO PICK UP FEMALES – CARTHAGINIAN STYLE

We also have a record by Hanno the Navigator, a Carthaginian who seems to describe a trip to West Africa about 100 years later. On this journey he captured two 'incredibly hairy and barbarous' females. As these were totally intractable and savage, he had them killed and returned home with their skins. These 'savages' he called *gorillas* – as indeed these creatures are still called today.

THE DEEP SOUTH

While northern Africa was well known to the Greeks and the Romans, who lived and farmed on its shores, few attempts were made to penetrate the trackless wastes of the Sahara, though some intrepid explorers may have made it as far as Timbuktu. Here is one such journey, told in his own inimitable way by Herodotus:

What I'm going to tell you now comes from a certain citizen of Cyrene [west of Egypt in Africa]. Once while he was visiting the oracular shrine of Amun, he fell in with Etearchus, the Ammonian king, and in random conversation they started talking about the Nile, and how no one had ever found its source. Etearchus … told the following tale. Some wild young men … drew lots for five of them to explore the desert parts of Libya, and boldly try to go into the interior where no man had gone before … The young men were accordingly sent off on their mission by their comrades, well-equipped with supplies of water and food.

They … finally entered the desert region, which they began to cross, travelling from east to west. They reached a vast waste of sand across which they journeyed for many days. At last they came to a plain where they observed trees were growing. They headed for the trees, and seeing fruit on them, they immediately started picking it. While they were doing this a number of men came up. These men were shorter than the average, and they made the travellers prisoner and carried them off. The Nasamonians could not understand a word of their tongue, nor did these people have any idea of the language of the travellers. They were taken … to a town. Everyone in this town was as short as the men who had led them there, and their skins were black. A great river, full of crocodiles, flowed past the town running from west to east. HERODOTUS, *THE HISTORIES*, 2.32

'Semper aliquid novi Africam adferre' (Africa always brings something new).
This quote from Pliny the Elder shows the fascination with Africa, also illustrated in this picture from a house in Pompeii.

FROM REFUGEE TO CONQUEROR

Mithridates, the first-century BC king of Pontus, was a formidable character. Once, his ship was in danger of foundering in a storm when a pirate ship turned up. Mithridates immediately persuaded the pirates not only to rescue him, but also to tow his ship to a friendly port.

Defeated by the Romans in 66–65 BC, Mithridates fled into the barbarous and uncharted wastelands of Scythia on the Black Sea, an area that the Mediterranean nations regarded in much the same way as Victorian explorers did 'Darkest Africa'. Pompey, the Roman general, attempted a pursuit, but withdrew on finding the tribesmen, weather and terrain uniformly hostile.

The historian Appian reports that despite these obstacles Mithridates 'pushed on through strange and warlike Scythian tribes, sometimes by permission, sometimes by force, so respected and feared was he'.

Among those who were congratulating themselves on seeing the last of Mithridates was his faithless son Menchares, who had defected to the Romans in exchange for keeping his kingdom of the Bosporus in the modern Crimea.

Exactly how he did it will never be known, but Mithridates survived the 500-mile journey to his son's kingdom. On the way he gathered an army from the wild peoples of the region and arrived like an avenging fury.

Silver tetradrachm of Mithridates. A coin such as this represented a week's pay for a soldier.

FOOD MILES

While we may think of the ancient world as embodying the ecologically sound principles of local production, in fact many of the ingredients consumed in Rome had travelled considerable distances. Indeed, in many cases the nations who consumed the materials and those who produced them didn't even know that the other existed. This was especially true of spices – cassia, cloves, nutmeg and ginger – which came all the way from southern China, or even from Indonesia. They were bundled with other exotic products such as silk, whose rarity made the fantastic cost of export worthwhile.

Lemons were new and exotic products to citizens of the early Roman empire.

From the Jade Gate in China, caravans carrying the spices set out to Bokara and Samarkand along the fabulous Silk Road (which was in fact a series of routes that shifted according to prevailing military and economic conditions). The spices were traded in local markets and resold, always at a profit, always moving west.

Some ended in India, to join other products imported by sea from eastern islands. These various spices were then loaded onto spice freighters – ships that also did a booming trade in pepper – at the ports of Bacare and Nelcynda, possibly in modern-day Kerala. (Even today Roman coins used in this trade are still unearthed in the Deccan.) The freighters then sailed along the coast, across the Red Sea and unloaded their goods at Mussolon in Egypt. Another caravan transferred the goods to Alexandria, and from there to Rome. Here, halfway across the planet from where they were grown, the spices were used to flavour wine and delicacies such as peacocks' brains and stuffed sows' udders.

TRADE GOODS

Apart from spices, other goods from faraway parts ended up in Rome – exotic trade products included:

Teak, rhinoceros horns, sandalwood, Chinese lacquer-ware, amber, tortoiseshell, flax, frankincense, cardamom seed, leopard-skin, Persian slippers, incense.

The biblical book of Revelation says that when Rome is destroyed there will no longer be a market for: 'cargoes of gold, silver, precious stones and pearls; fine linen, purple, silk and scarlet cloth; every kind of citron wood, and articles of all sorts made of ivory, costly wood, bronze, iron and marble; the cargoes of cinnamon and spice, of incense, myrrh and frankincense, of wine and olive oil, of fine flour and wheat; cattle and sheep; horses and carriages; and the bodies and souls of men.' *REVELATION* 18.12

INTRODUCING ELITHIO

Elithio Phoitete [literally the 'idiot student'] and a friend are on a journey. Elithio steps off the road for a call of nature, and returns to find that his friend has not waited, but has written on a nearby milestone – 'Catch me up'. Indignantly, Elithio scribbles:
'No, you wait for me!'

TRADITIONAL JOKE FROM ANCIENT GREECE

THE FOUR FURTHEST CORNERS OF THE ROMAN EMPIRE

North Lindum Damniorum, on the Antonine wall in modern Scotland

East Selucia-on-Tigris, just north of Babylon (very briefly supplanted by Dwin in Armenia in the reign of the emperor Trajan)

South Pselchis, just beyond the first cataract of the Nile

West Olisipo, on a peninsula in modern Portugal

ROMAN ROADS

Italy

The Appian Way Brundisium to Rome (362 miles/582 km)

The Via Salaria Castrum Trumentum on the Adriatic to Rome (152 miles/244 km)

Via Flaminia Rimini to Rome (205 miles/330 km)

Via Postumia Genua to Aquelia (Aquelia is near modern Venice and proves that not all roads lead to Rome) (192 miles/308 km)

Britain

Watling Street Dover to London (95 miles/153 km)

Ermine Street London to York (200 miles/320 km)

Stane Street London to Chichester (57 miles/92 km)

Fosse Way The mouth of the river Axe to Lincoln (220 miles/350 km)

Others

Via Egnatia Extended the Appian Way from Apollonia in Greece all the way to the Black Sea (about 700 miles/1,100 km)

Via Trajana Emesa in Syria to Palmyra (105 miles/167 km)

Via Augusta From Gaul to Gades (Cádiz), in Spain (455 miles/732 km)

A Roman road reaches the gates of a city, probably in the Greek east.

GOING ON HOLIDAY? SECOND-HAND
ROMAN VEHICLES FOR ALL OCCASIONS

Benna.

Arcera Four-wheeler, hybrid power: can be drawn by horses or slaves

Plaustrum Solid, primitive, no axle, needs lots of grease to keep the wheels turning

Benna Farm cart, no springs, no upholstery, no frills

Pilentrum Used for transporting Vestal Virgins

Thensa Chariots of the gods, used to carry statues of deities from their temples to watch the games

Essendum Celtic-style vehicle, generally a chariot type

Quadriga.

Chamulius Single-horse vehicle. Basically a first-century hansom cab

Quadriga War chariot drawn by four horses abreast. Imperial favourite

Postellum A light carriage for children or underweight ladies

Raeda Long-haul people carrier, suitable for overnight sleeping

Birota Two-wheeler, all-purpose runabout

Arcera.

DUNROMAN

The Roman army featured many journeys by individuals that collectively describe a huge series of peregrinations across the length and breadth of Rome's empire – and often far beyond its boundaries. Most poignant are those that end at the tombstones of legionaries and auxiliary soldiers who died hundreds, or even thousands, of miles from home. There is, for example, Longinus Sdapeze of the Thracian cavalry. Born in Sardica (modern Sofia, capital of Bulgaria), he ended up buried in Britain near Colchester. Gaius Saufeius of the Ninth Legion was from Heraclea (either in Greece or Asia Minor) but finished his days, aged 44, in Lincoln. On the other hand, Ulpius Enubico of the *Ala Britannorum* appears to have gone in the opposite direction, being buried at Intercisa, Pannonia Inferior (in modern Hungary).

Specialist units such as heavy cavalry and archers were particularly likely to be swept far from their homes by the tides of empire – as was the case for Hyperanor of the *Cohors I Sagittariorum*, a Cretan archer who was buried in upper Germany. The Romans also believed that some of the prisoners from their disastrous expedition into Parthia in 53 BC ended up serving as garrison troops in the east of the Parthian empire near what are now the western borders of China. In the 1950s, the excellently named sinologist Homer H. Dubs proposed that the blue-eyed blonds who occasionally crop up in the Chinese town of Liqian may be the descendants of Gallic cavalrymen whom the Roman general Crassus took east with him in his failed invasion attempt.

Tombstone showing a Roman trooper trampling ~~Gaulish soldier beneath his hor~~*se's hooves.*

TRAVELLERS' DISPATCHES

The sky is obscured by almost non-stop rain and cloud, though it never gets bitterly cold ... the soil will produce all the usual crops, and a lot of them. These grow quickly, but ripen slowly. Both effects have the same cause – both air and soil are excessively damp.

ROMAN VIEW OF BRITAIN IN TACITUS, *AGRICOLA*, 12

We set out with Attila for the northern parts of the country ... [we travelled] along a level road on a plain and encountered navigable rivers – the greatest of these, apart from the Danube, were the Drecon, Tigas and Tiphesas. We crossed these in monoxyles, which are boats made from one piece of wood, used by the peoples who live alongside the river. The smaller rivers we crossed on rafts that the barbarians [Huns] carry about with them on carts.

FROM THE TRAVEL DIARY OF PRISCUS, ON HIS EMBASSY TO
ATTILA THE HUN, C. AD 455

On my voyage from Asia, as I was sailing from Aegina towards Megara, I began to consider the places on each side of me. Behind me was Aegina, in front Megara, on my right Piraeus, on my left Corinth. All towns which once flourished greatly, but now lay before my eyes in ruin and decay.

SULPICIUS RUFUS, *CONSOLATION TO CICERO* AD FAM., 5.4

Merchant ships coming into harbour near Rome, from the relief of
Portus Torlonia.

After three months we put out to sea in a ship that had wintered
on the island. It was an Alexandrian ship with the figurehead of
the twin gods Castor and Pollux. We put in at Syracuse and stayed
there three days. From there we set sail and arrived at Rhegium.
The next day the south wind came up, and on the following day
we reached Puteoli. ... And so we came to Rome.

ACTS OF THE APOSTLES 27: 11–14

———

Floronius, immunis* *of the 7th Legion, came here, where the*
women did not know of him. Only six women came to know,
not enough for such a stallion.

GRAFFITO FROM POMPEII, CIL 8767
* see p. 132

———

Opposite *Greek warship, left, and merchant ship, right.*

THE SEVEN WONDERS OF THE ANCIENT WORLD

The 'Seven Wonders' were based upon the mystical number seven. (For the same reason Rome is said to have had seven hills, whereas the real number could arguably be four or ten.) There was no agreement as to what the Seven Wonders were, and rival lists circulated; the modern seven only became definitive long after most of them had vanished. Nevertheless, thousands of years ago, each of these wonders already attracted a substantial tourist trade.

1 THE GREAT LIGHTHOUSE AT ALEXANDRIA

Built in the third century BC, this was not originally a lighthouse, but was designed simply as a landmark (*pharos* in Greek) to help ships get their bearings on the flat Egyptian coast. It took another 300 years for the Romans to add a fire and a mirror that made the landmark visible at night – by some reports for up to 35 miles (56 km) out to sea. The lighthouse was finally destroyed by earthquakes in the fourteenth century AD.

2 THE HANGING GARDENS OF BABYLON

This wonder was built in about 600 BC by Nebuchadnezzar II to console his Medean wife, who missed the hills of her homeland. The gardens were a series of arched vaults and rather than 'hanging', grew on terraces. 'The chequered foundations are hollowed out. These are covered so deep with earth that very large trees could grow there,' reports the ancient writer Strabo (*Geography*, 16.5). Like the Great Lighthouse, the Hanging Gardens were eventually destroyed in an earthquake.

3 THE COLOSSUS OF RHODES

A 'colossus' was technically any statue larger than life, making the

The Great Lighthouse at Alexandria as it may have looked in Roman times.

Colossus of Rhodes almost overqualified for its name. It stood 110 ft (33 m) high – for comparison the Statue of Liberty is only 10 ft (3 m) taller – and was a wonder of engineering, art and sculpture all rolled into one. Representing the sun god Helios and commissioned to celebrate the survival of the city-state after a particularly difficult siege, work on the statue started in about 304 BC. The designer, Chares of Lindos, used material left over from the siege for the statue, which he cast in sections, starting from the feet and working upwards. The final result stood beside the harbour rather than straddling its entrance. It was destroyed 56 years later in an earthquake. (Observant readers will have spotted a trend here.) 'Even while it is fallen', wrote Pliny several centuries later, 'it arouses our wonder and admiration.' Eventually the remains were sold to a Jewish trader from Edessa who needed 900 camels to carry away the stones.

4. THE STATUE OF ZEUS AT OLYMPIA

From humble beginnings in 776 BC the Olympics rapidly became *the* sporting event of the ancient world. Consequently the organizers wanted something particularly special for their new temple of Zeus, so

A woodcut of the Statue of Zeus at Olympia.

they commissioned Phidias of Athens to create a monumental statue of the god. The final result, showing Zeus on his throne, was 40 ft (12 m) tall and 22 ft (6 m) wide, and took up all the space on the western side of the temple. 'If Zeus were to stand, he would demolish his home,' remarked Strabo. The statue was made of gold and ivory, the latter needing constant maintenance. Rumour had it that the name of Phidias' lover Pantarces was engraved on the god's little finger. Zeus outlived the Olympics, which were abolished as a pagan festival in late antiquity. The statue was moved to Constantinople where it was destroyed in a fire in AD 462.

5 THE TEMPLE OF ARTEMIS AT EPHESUS

In the sixth century BC, rulers competed with one another to see who could build the biggest temple; nobody, however, could match the achievements of the fabulously wealthy Croesus of Lydia, whose temple to Artemis measured 350 ft (100 m) long by 180 ft (55 m) in width. It stood for almost 200 years, but was burned down (supposedly on the very night that Alexander the Great was born) by a raving egomaniac so that 'his name would live forever'. In keeping with the tradition of many ancient writers, that name will not be mentioned here.

6 THE TOMB OF MAUSOLUS

When Mausolus, king of Halicarnassus, died in 353 BC, his sister and his wife were doubly heartbroken – after all, they were the same person. Artemisia (for that was her name) spared no expense in building her husband-brother a tomb, and she soon had the greatest designers and sculptors in the known world working on a hilltop just outside the royal capital. Although she died before the tomb was complete, the team decided to complete the work as a tribute to the king and also because they knew they were making something really special (says Pliny). The tomb was destroyed by earthquakes (surprise!) in the fourteenth century. The Crusaders soon vandalized the remaining parts, which were later scooped up and stashed in the British Museum. However, Mausolus was indeed immortalized, as any grand tomb is today called a 'mausoleum'.

7 THE GREAT PYRAMID AT GIZA

The grandaddy of all the wonders, this was built long before the others, in about 2500 BC. When Herodotus came to gape at it in 450 BC, it was already two millennia old. It stands 481 ft (150 m) high, and contains more building material than the Empire State Building – an estimated 2,250,000 stone blocks, each weighing over two tons. This gives the pyramid a permanence and solidity unequalled by any other building on earth (and fairly earthquake resistant).

A reconstruction of part of the Tomb of Mausolus at Halicarnassus.

EXOTIC FOREIGNERS

Nomads inhabit the eastern region of Libya. This is low-lying and sandy up to the Triton river; but west of this is well-farmed. There are many mountains and woodlands full of wild beasts. Here one finds huge snakes and lions, and elephants, bears and asps, horned donkeys and dog-headed men.
HERODOTUS, *THE HISTORIES*, 4.191

The dog-headed men (Cynocephali) were not baboons, for the ancients knew these well, but a strange race of humans. Pliny the Elder, in his *Natural History* (8.200 ff), lists these along with the following strange folk who inhabit the ends of the earth:

- **The Monopods** who have only one leg and a large foot, and can move amazingly fast, and on hot days lie on their backs and use their foot as a parasol
- **The Machyles** who are not merely bisexual, but assume either sex
- **The Blemmyae** who have no heads but faces set into their chests

THE SINGING STATUE OF MEMNON

A colossal statue of Memnon (Amenhotep III) at Thebes in Egypt was split by an earthquake in 27 BC. Thereafter it would 'sing' in the mornings as cool air expanded from the cracks in the stone. It became a major tourist attraction for the Romans, and even emperors used to visit. In AD 199 the emperor Septimius Severus decided to fix the earthquake damage, and so inadvertently stopped the statue's song.

Sorry landlord, we wet the bed. I know we shouldn't have,
but if you want to know why – there was no chamber pot.

APOLOGY FROM TWO TRAVELLERS ON THE DOOR OF THE
INN OF THE MULE-DRIVERS IN POMPEII, CIL 4957

ELITHIO AGAIN

Elithio Phoitete is travelling with his slaves in a ship. As a massive storm blows up and the ship threatens to sink and drown everyone on board, Elithio tells his slaves: 'Stop wailing like that! I've freed you in my will!'

TRADITIONAL JOKE FROM ANCIENT GREECE

THE SHIP

O ship, new waves will take you back to sea again.
What do you think you are doing?
Take courage, and head straight for safe haven.

You are made of the pines of Pontus, the daughter of a noble
  wood,
But don't boast of your ancestry – past fame is now useless
  to you.
The cautious sailor won't rely on that stern, be it painted
  ever so prettily.

Take care, or you are fated to become the sport of the winds.
And you, once a cause of so much pain and grief, but now
  my love and care,
Stay away from the treacherous seas and currents of the
  shining Cyclades.

HORACE, *ODES*, 1.14

*Merchant ship, from a relief on
a merchant's tomb at Pompeii.*

II

MILITARY
MISCELLANY

War in antiquity was a serious business, and a major occupation of most able-bodied males in ancient Greece. Even with the greater professionalism that the Romans brought to warfare, the oddities of chance or a bit of lateral thinking could bring chaos to the best-organized battlefield.

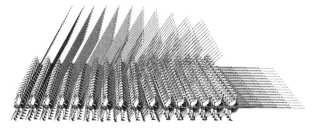

Phalanx going into action.

The Cats of War

When Cambyses II, king of Persia, invaded Egypt in 525 BC, he had clearly done his research. At the Battle of Pelusium his soldiers advanced on the Egyptian archers each carrying a cat. This effectively neutralized the Egyptians, who were terrified of injuring one of these revered beasts – and the Persians easily won the battle. Other reports suggest that, rather than carrying live cats, the soldiers painted images of Bast, the Egyptian cat goddess, on their shields. Either way, Bast got her revenge, for Cambyses later committed suicide when rebels in Persia made his position hopeless.

A Slight Miscalculation

Philip V of Macedon was an experienced campaigner who knew the value of speed. When he decided to storm the city of Larissa in central Greece, he did not want the inhabitants to know about it until it was all over. He brought up his army unnoticed, and at his signal his assault troops rushed at the unsuspecting city, carrying siege ladders with which to swarm over the wall. Sadly for the attackers, someone had blundered, and the ladders stopped about 6 ft (2 m) short of the top of the walls. While the bemused defenders hurriedly got their act together, the furious Macedonians abandoned their useless ladders and skulked off. Philip eventually took the city, but he had to do it the hard way.

DIRTY TRICKS IN FRONTINUS

Frontinus, later Rome's master of aqueducts, collected a set of military anecdotes, *Stratagems*, for use while he was campaigning in Britain. Here are some extracts:

Cimon, the Athenian general, intended to attack a certain city in Caria [in Asia Minor]. So, concealed by the night, his men set fire to a deeply revered temple of Diana and also to a sacred grove outside the walls. The inhabitants rushed out of town to tackle the blaze, and Cimon captured the city, which was now empty of defenders.
STRATAGEMS, 2.5

Metellus [consul in 143 BC and therefore probably Quintus Caecilius Metellus Macedonicus] was fighting in Spain. The enemy had pitched camp on low-lying ground so Metellus had his men divert a river so that it flowed down into the camp. He then stationed his men in ambush to cut down the enemy as they fled in panic from the sudden flood. *STRATAGEMS*, 7.3

Cleisthenes of Sikyon [585 BC] cut the water pipes leading into the town of the Crisaeans [modern-day Kirrha] until the townspeople were in great distress from thirst. Then he restored their water, which he had now contaminated with hellebore [a violent natural laxative]. After drinking the water, the inhabitants were so debilitated by diarrhoea that Cleisthenes was easily able to defeat them.
STRATAGEMS, 7.6

Epaminondas of Thebes was campaigning in Arcadia. During a feast day [when there was no fighting] many enemy townswomen were walking around outside the city walls. So he dressed up a number of his men in women's clothing and told them to mingle with the crowd. Under this disguise the men joined the others who were allowed through the gates at nightfall. They seized the gates and threw them open for their fellow soldiers.
STRATAGEMS, 2.7

LIVING LEGACY

*The same Epaminondas [p. 26] was the first ever to lead the Thebans
to victory against the Spartans, not once, but twice. As he lay dying
from a spear-wound someone tearfully said: 'And you have no son to
carry on your name.' 'By the gods, I do not', he replied, 'but I leave
two daughters – victory at Leuctra and victory at Mantinea.'*

PARAPHRASED FROM DIODORUS, 15.87

THE MULTI-FUNCTION TORTOISE

The famous Roman *testudo* – a 'tortoise' of shields used to protect
legionaries from missiles coming from all directions – had other uses
as well. Livy tells of a time in the second century BC when the legions
were campaigning in Greece. Their enemies were sheltering behind a
wall – only 6 ft (2 m) high, but nevertheless a considerable inconven-
ience. The legion hardly broke stride. The first rank of men rushed
straight at the wall, raised their shields over their heads, and slammed
the edges against the wall. The next rank arrived, crouched, and laid
their shields at an angle along their backs. The next rank knelt, also
with angled shields. The remainder of the legion thundered up the
improvised ramp, met the enemy face to face and (as the legions were
wont to do) cut the enemy to pieces.

Romans in
testudo
*formation attack
an enemy
fortification
defended by
Dacian warriors.*

WITH ENEMIES LIKE THESE, WHO NEEDS FRIENDS?

The Roman consuls greet King Pyrrhus.

We are greatly disturbed by your continued iniquities, and intend to treat you as an enemy. But we want you personally to remain safe so that we can defeat you in battle. Your friend Nicias has come to us, asking for a reward if he were to assassinate you. It seems proper to inform you, in case something like this happens and other nations think we connived at it. We therefore advise you to conduct yourself with care. PARAPHRASE OF A LETTER TO PYRRHUS OF EPIRUS WHILE HE WAS INVADING ITALY C. 280 BC, QUOTED IN AULUS GELLIUS, *ATTIC NIGHTS*, 3.8

MARTIAL ARDOUR

Greek nations used horns and trumpet blasts to fire up the martial ardour of their soldiers before they charged into the fray. All except the Spartans. They used pipes and flutes to calm their men down.

AULUS GELLIUS, *ATTIC NIGHTS*, 1.11

WEAPONS OF MASS DESTRUCTION USED IN MIDDLE EAST FLASHPOINT

Evidence of poison gas created by burning a mixture of bitumen and sulphur has been discovered at Dura-Europos, a Roman fortress town that was subjected to a ferocious siege by the Sassanid Persians in around AD 250. Archaeologists discovered a group of 20 Romans who died in an underground tunnel without any signs of a struggle. A closer examination of the site revealed that these were Roman sappers (see p. 129) who were digging a counter-mine to prevent their Persian counterparts from digging under the Roman walls.

It seems the Persians discovered this tunnel, and prepared their noxious chemical weapon as a response. 'The Romans would have been unconscious within seconds and dead in minutes,' said the archaeologist who figured out the nefarious Persian trick.

Another use of biological warfare was by the people of Hatra (in modern-day Iraq), where the defenders of the city poured flaming naphtha (a sort of ancient napalm) over the siege engines of the Roman emperor Septimius Severus. When the legionaries attacked the walls they were bombarded with clay jars filled with scorpions.

TYPES OF ANCIENT GREEK SOLDIER

Hoplite The heavy infantryman who was the standard soldier in the fifth century BC

Peltast A more lightly armoured soldier who protected the sides of the hoplite phalanx

Toxotes Archer. His equivalent on horseback was a hippotoxotes

Hippikon Cavalryman

Hatairoi The 'Companions'. Alexander the Great's shock troops, consisting of lance-armed heavy cavalry

Phalangite A soldier who fought in the phalanx, armed with a light shield and a 16-ft (5-m) spear

Acrobolos A skirmisher who fought with light missile weapons

Xenagia A mercenary

LACONIC OBSERVATIONS

Athenian to a Spartan: *The Athenians are no mean warriors.*
See how many Spartans have been slain around Athens.
Spartan to Athenian: *And so few Athenians have died*
anywhere near Sparta.

A visitor to Athens admiring a mural of Athenians
in battle: *These Athenians are ferocious warriors.*
Spartan bystander: *They are, in paint.*

MILITARY HEAVY GOODS TRANSPORTER (BIPED, MK I)

'What is a legionary but a beast of burden?' asks the historian Josephus rhetorically. Using some very approximate figures (legionary equipment was never fully standardized), one of Trajan's legionaries might go for a day's march of 20 miles with:

- **Helmet** 5 ½ lbs (2.5 kg)
- *Pilum* 5 lbs (2.3 kg)
- **Shield** 20 lbs (9 kg)
- **Armour** 16 lbs (7.3 kg)
- *Gladius* 3 ½ lbs (1.5 kg)
- **Digging tool** 4 lbs (1.8 kg)
- **Three days' food and some drinking water** 7 lbs (3.2 kg)
- **Mess-tin, dagger, personal kit** 3 lbs (1.4 kg)
- **Cloak (dry weight)** 2 ½ lbs (1 kg)

- **Total** 66 ½ lbs (30 kg)

unless the legionary was also carrying one or two wooden stakes to put on the ramparts of the camp that night – in which case add at least another 5 lbs (2.3 kg).

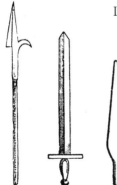

Legionaries of the early Roman army used to have much of this kit carried on a donkey, but at the end of the second century BC the general Gaius Marius decreed every soldier should carry his own kit. Thereafter legionaries wryly referred to themselves as 'Marius' mules'.

Above *'Gallic' helmet.* **Left** Sparum *and two* spathas.

NICKNAMES OF LEGIONS

Most Roman legions had an identifying nickname – essential when the vagaries of time had given some different legions the same unit number (for example, I Italica and I Adiutrix). Some of the nicknames include:

Fidelis 'Faithful' – usually given either to strengthen the loyalty of wavering legions, or to legions that had shown exceptional loyalty – generally by refusing to join a popular revolt

Rapax 'Grasping' or 'seizing' – as in how a predator captures its victim

Gemina 'Twin' – used when two legions (such as the two thirteenth legions) were combined into a single entity

Italica 'Italian' – indicating that the legion was raised entirely from Italian citizens

Valeria 'The brave' – given to a legion that performed exceptionally well, as with XX Valeria Victrix

Adiutrix 'Supportive' – these were legions originally raised in emergencies

Primigenia 'The firstborn' – these were originally planned to be a new kind of legion, but in the end they settled into the standard model

Stone commemorating the Legio II Augusta.

PEACE TERMS

After Alexander invaded the Persian empire, King Darius offered him generous terms for peace. He would pay Alexander 10,000 talents, give him the areas west of the Euphrates and he would give his own daughter to Alexander in marriage. Alexander consulted advisors and his general Parmenion said, 'If I were Alexander, I would accept these terms.' Alexander answered, 'I would, if I were Parmenion.'

FAMOUS LAST WORDS – NO. 1

The enemy prepared to charge ... 'But Demetrius will come to my rescue,' said Antigonus. And in this hope he persisted to the last, looking out on every side for his son's approach, until he was struck down by a whole swarm of darts.

PLUTARCH DESCRIBES ANTIGONUS MONOPHTHALMUS AT THE BATTLE OF IPSUS IN 301 BC, AS HE DISCOVERS THAT HIS SON HAS BEEN UNAVOIDABLY DETAINED. PLUTARCH, *LIFE OF DEMETRIUS*, 29

HANNIBAL, ENEMY OF ROME

Hannibal was perhaps Rome's most fearsome opponent, and almost brought the empire to its knees in the third century BC. Polybius tells this story of how it all began, during the First Punic War (264–241 BC):

The omens were favourable, Hamilcar [Hannibal's father] ... ordered the others attending the sacrifice to step away somewhat, and called Hannibal over. He asked Hannibal gently if he wanted to come with him on the expedition [to Spain]. Boy-like, Hannibal accepted with delight ... So his father took him by the hand and led him up to the altar. He told Hannibal to put his hand on the body of the sacrificial victim and swear never to be the friend of the Romans. POLYBIUS, *HISTORIES*, 3.9

HANNIBAL CROSSES THE ALPS

The new snow was soft, but it had fallen on the top of old snow which had been there since the previous winter ... Therefore Hannibal ordered the soldiers to the grinding work of building a path along the cliff. In one day he had made a passage wide enough for the pack-train and horses. He took these across immediately, and made camp on a snow-free pasture where the animals could graze. The Numidians worked in shifts at building up the path. After three

Right *Bust of Hannibal.* **Opposite** *Coin showing the (now extinct) North African elephant.*

days he managed with great difficulty to get the elephants across, but hunger had sorely reduced the animals' condition. POLYBIUS, *HISTORIES*, 3.53

ESCAPING A ROMAN TRAP

The enemy had such a good position [blocking the passes to Apulia in Italy] that there was no hope of breaking out. Realizing they were surrounded and trapped the soldiers became demoralized and terrified. In these circumstances, Hannibal was reduced to using trickery. He had 2,000 oxen in his camp, and he ordered torches or small bundles of wood to be tied to their horns.

At evenfall he had the beasts driven toward the enemy outposts that commanded the heights overlooking the valley ... The oxen at first kept a slow orderly pace, and with their lighted heads resembled an army marching by night ... This spectacle astonished the Romans on guard upon the heights. Seeing the 'enemy' approaching in number from all sides they abandoned their outposts and hurriedly withdrew to the main camp in the hills.

As soon as they were gone, Hannibal's light infantry, as ordered, seized their positions and shortly afterwards the whole army, with its baggage, advanced safely through the passes. PLUTARCH, *LIFE OF FABIUS*, 6

HIGHLY DESIRABLE EQUIPMENT

When he was an old man and in exile, Hannibal came into the service of Antiochus, king of Seleucia. Antiochus showed Hannibal his army, with its lavishly equipped and richly decorated soldiers, and proudly asked if these would be 'enough for the Romans'. 'I believe so,' replied Hannibal. Then he added: 'But the Romans are very greedy.'

HANNIBAL'S CLASHES WITH ROME

1 River Ticinus

Date November 218 BC

Opponent Publius Scipio

Rome 4,000 cavalry, light troops

Carthage 6,000 cavalry

Victor Carthage – narrow win

Roman casualties 1,000 dead (rough estimate)

2 River Trebbia

Date December 218 BC

Opponent Tiberius Sempronius

Rome 36,000 infantry, 4,000 cavalry

Carthage 29,000 infantry, 11,000 cavalry, 35 elephants

Victor Carthage – narrow win

Roman casualties 8,000 dead (rough estimate)

3 Lake Trasimene

Date June 217 BC

Opponent C. Flaminus

Rome 25,000 infantry

Carthage 60,000 infantry

Victor Carthage – decisive win

Roman casualties 15,000 dead, approx. 9,500 prisoners

4 Cannae

Date August 216 BC

Opponent Terentius Varro, Aemilius Paullus

Rome 80,000 infantry, 6,000 cavalry

Carthage 40,000 infantry, 10,000 cavalry

Victor Carthage – decisive win

Roman casualties 60,000 dead, 4,000 prisoners

5 Zama

Date October 202 BC

Opponent Scipio Africanus

Rome 29,000 infantry, 6,000 cavalry

Carthage 36,000 infantry, 4,000 cavalry, 80 elephants

Victor Rome – decisive win

Carthaginian casualties 20,000 dead

CAESAR IN BRITAIN

CONQUERED WHERE?

Caesar did indeed say 'veni, vidi, vici' (I came, I saw, I conquered). But he did not say it about Britain, where he came, had a bit of trouble with British chariots, and eventually called off operations altogether due to bad weather. The 'veni, vidi, vici' described his (very brief) campaign against Pharnaces of Pontus, in Asia Minor.

A TRICKY MOMENT ON D-DAY

Our ships [carrying the Romans to Britain] were so big that they could go only in deep water. Our soldiers were faced with the prospect of leaping from them in heavy armour into waves of unknown depth, and standing there to meet the enemy. They hesitated, mainly because the sea seemed so deep. So the standard bearer of the tenth legion, after a prayer to the gods that things would work out well for the legion, shouted: 'Jump, soldiers, unless you want to see your eagle in the hands of the enemy. Because I personally intend to do my duty for my motherland and my general.' After this declamation, he leapt overboard and proceeded to carry his eagle towards the enemy. Our men told each other not to allow such shame to fall on them, and all jumped off the ship. CAESAR, *THE GALLIC WAR*, 4.25–6

THOSE PESKY CHARIOTS

They [the Britons] fight in their chariots like this. First, they fly about in all directions throwing weapons. When they have worked themselves into the troops, the Britons leap from their chariots and fight on foot. Meanwhile the charioteers pull back a bit from the battle, and place themselves so that, if their masters are outnumbered or overpowered, they have available a quick line of retreat to their own side.

So in battle the chariots have the speed of cavalry and the firmness of infantry. They practise daily and are so expert that, even going down steep hills they can brake at full speed, turn instantly, run along the pole [between the horses], and stand on the yoke, and then rush at high speed back into their chariots. CAESAR, *THE GALLIC WAR*, 4.33

Scythe Chariots

So Caesar thought he had it bad? In the Middle East some chariots had huge scythes affixed to the wheels. In the right conditions these chariots had a devastating effect on enemy infantry, such as these unfortunate Bithynian foot-soldiers who were hit by the scythe chariots of Mithridates of Pontus.

The chariots were driven at high speed into the Bithynian ranks. Some men were sliced in two within an eyeblink, others were practically shredded. The army of Nicomedes saw men in two halves, yet still alive and breathing, others sliced to pieces, their mangled organs still hanging from the scythes. They had by no means lost the battle, yet the sight was so hideous that they were overcome with confusion, and fear disordered their ranks. APPIAN, *THE MITHRIDATIC WARS*, 3.18

Yet against experienced soldiers scythe chariots stood no chance. When the same chariots attacked veteran legionaries in Greece, the Romans simply opened their ranks to allow the chariots to thunder through and be finished off by strategically placed javelin-men at the back. Once the first wave had vanished into their ranks to be destroyed, the legionaries cheerfully asked for another attack, using the traditional shout of spectators at the Circus Maximus in Rome awaiting the next chariot race.

In the next battle the Pontic commander tried packing the chariots closer together. The Roman legionaries watched them charge. Then, just before the chariots hit, the soldiers of the front rank each stepped smartly sideways and back to reveal sharpened stakes carefully angled for maximum impalement. After this second catastrophic failure, scythe chariots were never again deployed in anger.

AN IMPERIAL PUT-DOWN

A character was boasting within earshot of Augustus of the battle in which he had received an unsightly scar on his face. The emperor gently advised him: 'Never look back when you are running away.'

THE DEFENCE OF PLATAEA

During the Peloponnesian War of 431–404 BC, the little city of Plataea was besieged by the Spartans. The attackers built a large earth ramp to take their army over the city walls, but the Plataeans, who made up in ingenuity what they lacked in numbers, knocked a hole in their own wall where the ramp was being built, and removed the earth from it as fast as it was being added.

Eventually the besiegers noticed this, and started putting the earth into large reed baskets to make it harder to pull through the hole in the wall. Yet still the mound grew inexplicably slowly. Eventually the attackers realized that the Plataeans had dug under the mound as well, and were removing earth from the bottom, so that the ramp subsided as fast as it grew.

FAMOUS LAST WORDS – NO. 2

If that's an army, they are too few. If it's a diplomatic embassy, they are too many.

TIGRANES THE GREAT OF ARMENIA, AT
TIGRANOCERTA IN 69 BC, SURVEYING
THE 12,000 ROMAN SOLDIERS WHO
WERE ABOUT TO TEAR APART HIS
ARMY OF SOME 135,000 MEN

ROMAN SIEGE BALLISTA

- **Range** 100–400 yards (90–350 m), depending on weight of shot
- **Propulsion** Elastic ropes of ox-sinew and women's hair
- **Height** 24 ½ ft (7.5 metres)
- **Length** 28 ft (8.5 metres)
- **Weight** 12 tons

So when they had cut down all the trees on the mountains around the city, and had piled up a huge heap of stones ... Vespasian set up around the city catapults for throwing stones and bolts. There were 160 of them, and on command they set about clearing the defenders from the walls. The bolt throwers did their work with a huge noise and the rock throwers hurled stones up to 60 lbs [27 kg] together with fire, and a positive storm of arrows ... So great was the force of that catapult that one of the men who stood by Josephus and was near the wall had his head taken off by one of these stones, and his skull was thrown well over 500 yards.

JOSEPHUS, *THE JEWISH WAR*, 7.8 ff

Catapult.

SHORT QUIPS BY CICERO – NO. 1

When Cicero saw Lentulus, his very short son-in-law, in armour complete with a very long sword, he asked:
'Who buckled Lentulus onto that sword?'

MACROBIUS, *SATURNALIA*, 3.2

SHORT QUIPS BY CICERO – NO. 2

Cicero's brother was no giant either. Cicero once saw a larger-than-life picture of his brother painted on a shield. As was customary with such pictures, this showed the subject from the waist up and was a case, Cicero reckoned, 'Where the half was greater than the whole'.

MACROBIUS, *SATURNALIA*, 3.3

DEFEATED BY DAWN

The year AD 69 saw no fewer than four claimants to the imperial Roman throne, each one being overthrown by the next. This was finally resolved during the second Battle of Cremona, when the eastern legions of Vespasian faced the Rhine legions of the then emperor Vitellius. The fight started in the evening and went on until dawn. At dawn, the soldiers of the Syrian third legion, who worshipped Helios, turned eastward and gave their habitual cries of greeting as their god rose above the horizon. The rest of their army assumed that they were greeting reinforcements, and attacked with extra vigour. The Vitellians, demoralized by the same belief, broke and fled, becoming the only army ever to have been beaten by the dawn.

ROMAN CROWNS FOR MILITARY ACHIEVEMENT

The Laurel Crown Worn by a Roman general in a triumphal procession

The Olive Crown For a triumphing general who was not actually at the victorious battle

The Myrtle Crown For a general who receives an ovation

The Grass Crown For saving a city under siege

The Oak Crown For saving the life of a fellow citizen in battle

The Mural Crown For the first man onto the walls of an enemy city

The Camp Crown For the first man over the ramparts of an enemy camp

The Naval Crown For the first to board an enemy ship

(The last three crowns were all of gold)

DIED IN ACTION

Pyrrhus, King of Epirus
After whom the Pyrrhic victory is named. Died in 272 BC when hit by a well-flung roof tile while attacking the city of Argos.

Leonidas, King of Sparta
Died in 480 BC while holding off the Persian army with his 300 Spartans at Thermopylae.

Lucius Postumius Albinus, Consul-elect of Rome
Killed by the Celts in 216 BC; his skull ended up being plated with gold and used as a drinking cup.

Claudius Marcellus
Consul known as 'the sword of Rome', killed fighting Hannibal in 208 BC.

Publius Cornelius Scipio
Father of Scipio Africanus, the conqueror of Hannibal, was killed in 211 BC while fighting Carthaginians in Spain.

Spartacus
Rebel and gladiator, was finally defeated in battle by Crassus in 71 BC.

Publius Licinius Crassus
Triumvir and the 'richest man in Rome', died in 53 BC at Carrhae, in the Middle East, while fighting the Parthians.

Valens
Roman emperor, killed by the Goths after losing the Battle of Adrianople in AD 378.

HEROES: THREE SUPER-SOLDIERS IN PLINY

THE MIGHTY JUNIUS
Junius Valens, a centurion in the Praetorian Guard of the divine Augustus, was accustomed to hold up wagons loaded with sacks until they were unloaded; with one hand he could hold back a chariot, standing firm against all the force of the horses. PLINY THE ELDER, *NATURAL HISTORY*, 7.203

THE HUMAN TELESCOPE

A man called Strabo during the [first] Carthaginian War would stand upon the promontory of Lilybaeum, in Sicily, and see the fleet coming out of the harbour of Carthage [in North Africa, about 100 miles (161 km) away]. He was even able to tell the number of warships. PLINY THE ELDER, *NATURAL HISTORY*, 7.205

THE INDESTRUCTIBLE SERGIUS

M. Sergius ... lost his right hand ... and he was wounded twenty-three times. Twice he was taken prisoner by Hannibal (for he did not serve against ordinary enemies), and twice he escaped from his bonds. Four times he fought with his left hand only, until two horses were killed under him. He made himself a right hand of iron, and he fought with it fastened to his arm. PLINY THE ELDER, *NATURAL HISTORY*, 7.213

THE PERILS OF LEADERSHIP

Fighting the Athenians was dangerous, leading them in battle even more so. Athens expected generals to lead from the front and was ruthless with those who did not come up to expectations. Here is what became of the Athenian leaders during the Peloponnesian War against Sparta and her allies in the fifth century BC.

Pericles Died of the plague in 430 BC

Cleon Died in 422 BC while fighting outside the city of Amphipolis

Demosthenes Captured and executed by the Syracusans in 415 BC after an unsuccessful Athenian siege

Nicias Commander along with Demosthenes, and shared his fate

Thucydides Failed to defeat the brilliant Spartan general Brasidas, and was exiled for his pains. Took up writing history instead

Theramenes One of the admirals who fought at the Battle of Arginusae. Though the Athenians were victorious, six of Theramenes' fellow generals were executed for not taking enough care of the fallen. He was executed soon after the end of the war for resisting the new oligarchic government

Alcibiades Exiled, restored and exiled once more, he was finally assassinated in 404 BC, either by the Spartans or the Persians

Conon Fled into exile after losing the Battle of Aegospotami, but survived the war

Thrasybulus A rival of Conon, he also survived the war, but was killed in a later one

BARBARIANS AT THE GATE

But which barbarians? A quick guide to the peoples who brought down the Roman empire for those who don't know their Alans from their Ostrogoths.

Sarmatian cavalry attack Romans.

Alans A tribe of warrior horsemen displaced from the Black Sea region by the Huns. They sought homes in Gaul, Spain and then Africa, fighting or allying with the native Roman citizenry according to circumstances.

Sarmatians Heavily armoured cavalrymen who had plagued the Romans from the first century AD onwards. As Rome's power weakened, they steadily regained land they had lost in Dacia and the northeastern frontier.

Huns Led by the formidable Attila ('the scourge of God'), these caused considerable distress even before they invaded Europe, for they drove before them the …

Ostrogoths A tribe from what is now the western Ukraine. These people eventually settled in Greece and the western Balkans before moving into Italy itself. They drove before them the …

Visigoths These people killed the emperor Valens at the Battle of Adrianople, and under their leader Alaric were the first to sack Rome since the Gauls almost 1,000 years before. The next tribe to sack Rome were the …

Vandals Who did it much more thoroughly than Alaric's half-hearted attempt, and so earned themselves an eternal place in the English language as mindless thugs.

Gepids A little-known Germanic tribe who fought Huns, Langobards, Romans and Ostrogoths, and generally lost to all of them. Were finally defeated by the Avars, yet another barbarian tribe from the east in 567, well after the fall of the western empire.

Franks Ended up in France.

Burgundians Ended up in Burgundy.

Langobards Ended up in Lombardy, north Italy.

Angles Ended up in Anglia, England.

Saxons Settled in most of the rest of England, combining with the Angles to become the Anglo-Saxons.

THE ATHENIANS BURY THEIR WAR DEAD

The bones of the dead are laid out in a tent raised for the purpose. Friends bring their relatives such offerings to the dead as they think appropriate. In the funeral procession, cypress coffins are carried on carriages, one for each tribe, and the bones of the dead are placed in the coffin of their tribe. Among these is carried one empty coffin – this is for those lost whose corpses could not be recovered. Anyone who wishes, citizen or not, can join in the procession. The female relatives are there, and wail at the burial. The dead are laid to rest in the public sepulchre at Kerameikos, the most beautiful part of the city, just outside the city walls. Those who fall in war are always buried here apart from those who died at Marathon. These, in recognition of their exceptional and extraordinary valour, were laid to rest where they fell. After the bodies have been interred, a speech in their honour is given by someone the people consider to be of outstanding wisdom and good character, after which all retire. THUCYDIDES, *THE PELOPONNESIAN WAR*, 2.34 ff

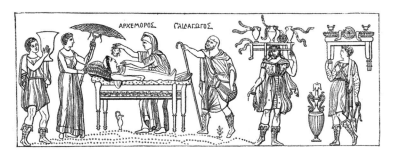

Greek funeral scene.

THE DOVES OF WAR

One of the earliest recorded uses of carrier pigeons to transmit military intelligence was by Decimus Brutus who was under siege by Mark Antony in the civil war of 43 BC.

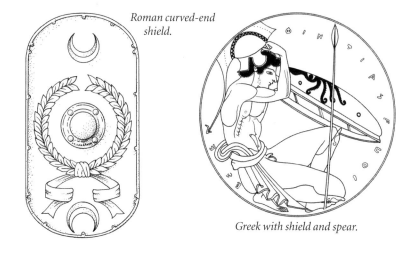

Roman curved-end shield.

Greek with shield and spear.

POETS ON THE RUN

Losing a shield was a major disgrace, as it meant that a warrior had dropped it, to flee all the faster from the battlefield. Hence the Spartan mother's famous warning as she equips her son for war: 'Come back with this shield, or on it' (shields were also used to carry corpses from the battlefield). Not everyone was quite so macho. Certainly not the poet and mercenary Archilochus:

> So some Thracian is delighted with the shield,
> Which, unwillingly I dumped beside some bush
> Well, to hell with it – I saved myself!
> Why should I care about a shield?
> I'll get another, just as good.
>
> ARCHILOCHUS FR 6 BD

Plutarch says Archilochus was ordered to leave town at one hour's notice when the Spartans became aware of his defeatist tripe. It did not stop Alcaeus writing to a friend in similar vein, however:

Alcaeus is safe, his weapons are not
The Athenians captured them and they hang
As trophies in the temple
Of their grey-eyed goddess.

ALCAEUS FR 428A

The poet Horace felt the same when he managed to avoid going down with the Republican cause in the Battle of Philippi:

I experienced Philippi with you
And the swift flight
My poor little shield abandoned
(Which was not good)
But virtue was broken
And even the brave and threatening
Were biting the dust
Swift Mercury carried me off in my terror.

(The reference to Mercury is a clever play on his role as the patron god of poets and his winged feet.)

Funeral monuments at Athens.

III

BIZARRE
BELIEFS

Not all Greeks and Romans were superstitious, but even
hardened scholars such as Pliny the Elder and Aristotle
believed some odd things – not because they were
credulous, but because travel was generally so restricted
and science was so little advanced that they had to rely
heavily on speculation and travellers' tales. Overall, the
ancient scholars did a good job in sorting the credible
from the incredible, and often reported the beliefs and
statements of others with due scepticism.

Medusa with her offspring, winged Pegasus and his brother
Chrysaor, from a bronze shield decoration, Olympia (see p. 53).

CURSE YOU!

At Aquae Sulis (Bath) in Britain Romans came to partake of the waters, just as the cream of English society would 1,600 years later. Minerva Sulis, goddess of the waters, was often called on by those seeking justice or vengeance. Over 100 little messages inscribed on lead have been retrieved after they were rolled up and cast into the waters in the belief that the goddess would take action accordingly. Here is a selection:

- May he who has stolen Vilbia from me become as liquid as water.
- I curse him who has stolen, who has robbed Deomiorix at his house. Whoever stole his property, the goddess is to find him. Let him buy it back with his blood or his own life.
- I curse him who has stolen my hooded cloak … may the goddess Sulis … not allow him sleep or children now and in the future, until he has brought my hooded cloak to her scared temple.
- To the goddess Sulis Minerva. I ask your most sacred majesty that you take vengeance on those who have wronged me, that you never permit them to sleep.
- I have given the goddess Sulis the six silver coins I have lost. She can get them from those listed below – Anniola, Saturninus, Senicanus.
- Whether man or woman, boy or girl, slave or free, whoever took my bronze urn is accursed forever … Let the perpetrator's own blood be spilled into the bowl.

DOGS IN ROMAN SUPERSTITION

Dog's blood, placed under the threshold of a house, keeps away evil spirits.

The gall bladder of a black male dog is an effective defence against magic.

The froth from the mouth of a mad dog is a powerful ingredient in magical concoctions.

The dog star (Sirius) rose with the sun in the hottest part of the year, and the Romans believe that its rays are added to the sun's to make things particularly hot. Hence the *caniculares dies* – or 'dog days' – of summer.

The howling of dogs presages a death.

Warts can be cured by a mixture of dog urine and mud.

A person suffering from illness might be cured if rubbed all over with a puppy (though the outlook thereafter for the puppy is not good).

A person suffering from illness might be cured if rubbed all over with a puppy (though the outlook thereafter for the puppy is not good).

The sacrifice of a rust-coloured dog would placate Robigo, the goddess of crop diseases, and save grain from a type of blight called 'rust'.

And a (dangerously incorrect) postscript from Aristotle: 'Rabies drives the animal mad, and any animal whatever, excepting man, will become infected if bitten by a dog so afflicted; the disease is fatal to the dog itself, and to any animal it may bite, man excepted.'
THE HISTORY OF ANIMALS, 9.22

READING THE GODS' MINDS

The Romans believed so firmly that the will of the gods could be interpreted by the flight or feeding pattern of birds that they had a class of priests (*augures*) the better to be able to interpret these. Indeed, augury was used to decide whether the first houses of Rome should be built on the Palatine or the Aventine hill. Other ways the gods made their will known was through the condition of the internal organs of a sacrificial animal – as determined by another class of priest called a *haruspex* (literally 'gut-gazer') – or through dreams.

*The Piacenza Liver, c. 100 BC.
A bronze model of a sheep's liver
is inscribed with points of
oracular significance .*

*Some facts will appear of an astounding nature, and, indeed,
incredible to many. Who, for instance, could ever believe in the
existence of the Ethiopians, if they hadn't actually seen them?*

PLINY THE ELDER, *NATURAL HISTORY*, 7.1

SEEING-EYE FLY

*The consul Mucianus suffered from the fear of losing his eyesight.
He sought to prevent this loss by carrying with him a live fly
in a white cloth. Happily, says the Elder Pliny, the fly did its job,
and Mucianus kept his eyesight.*

TALKING OF EYESIGHT ...

There was considerable debate among philosophers as to how seeing actually worked. Some, such as the Epicurians, felt that matter gave off a sort of 'skin' of light that was perceived by the eye. Others felt that the eye itself was the active agent, and used a kind of ray to see things, rather as a flashlight works in a dark room.

When Plato was lecturing on his theory of 'abstracts', Diogenes commented: 'I can see a table and a cup. I can't see a theoretical table or cup.' To which Plato replied: 'That's because your eyes can see the one type, but your mind fails to see the other.' DIOGENES LAËRTIUS, *LIVES AND OPINIONS OF EMINENT PHILOSOPHERS*, 6. 2

PLINY ON ASTRONOMY

Given that the Greeks and Romans had only intelligence and the naked eye to speculate about the cosmos, it is not surprising that they could be wildly inaccurate. What is astounding is that they were often right:

ON THE EXISTENCE OF OTHER WORLDS

It is madness to harass the mind, as some have done, with attempts to measure the world, and to publish these attempts; or, like others, to argue from their conclusions that there are innumerable other worlds, and ... if only one nature produced the whole, there will be so many suns and so many moons, and that each of them will have immense trains of other heavenly bodies. PLINY THE ELDER, *NATURAL HISTORY*, 2.1

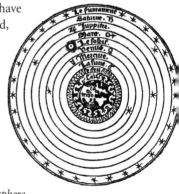

Ptolemy's order of the solar system, showing the planets with each nested in its own transparent sphere.

THE SIZE OF THE SUN

It is immeasurably huge. This you can tell from the following observation. Trees which are planted at the far limits of East and West, nevertheless cast shadows of the same proportions – though these trees are miles and miles apart, the sun appears in the same place, as though centred on either one.

PLINY THE ELDER, *NATURAL HISTORY*, 2.45

THE MOON AND PLANETS

Pliny was well aware that the world was round, and that it rotated on its axis every 24 hours. However, he believed that the planets rotated around the earth, from Saturn (the outermost) to Jupiter then Mars and finally – beneath the sun – the erratic and wandering Venus and tiny Mercury.

The moon, according to Pliny, is 126,000 stades away. This is about 15,000 miles (24,000 km) – an error of about 235,000 miles (380,000 km). Perhaps he should have paid more attention to Posidonius, whose estimate of two million stades – 250,000 miles – is pretty near spot on.

PLUTARCH ABHORS A VACUUM

*But above all, what is most absurd is what they say of the universe …
that [it] is neither a body nor bodiless … It is often said by
Chrysippus that there is beyond the world an infinite vacuum, and
that this infinity has neither beginning, middle, nor end.*

PLUTARCH, *AGAINST THE STOICS*, 30, AND
ON THE CONTRADICTIONS OF THE STOICS, 44

NUCLEAR PHYSICS IN AD 100

*What, therefore, these men principally object to the supporters of
[theories about] those indivisible bodies called atoms is this, that
neither do they wholly touch, nor does any part touch the other parts.*

PLUTARCH, *AGAINST THE STOICS*, 40

SINISTER SEVEN

*Diseases have greater violence on days which are made up of the
number seven ... and Varro does not fail to mention a fact which adds
to the power and influence of the number seven, namely, that those
who resolve to die of starvation meet their end on the seventh day.*

AULUS GELLIUS, *ATTIC NIGHTS*, 3.10

SUPERSTITIONS OF THE EMPEROR AUGUSTUS

Even the master of the Roman world had his particular foibles ...

- If he accidentally put his left shoe on his right foot, or vice versa, he considered it a bad sign.
- If there was a shower of rain when he was starting on a long journey, he thought it a good omen.
- He refused to begin a journey on the day after a market day.

BAD MOON RISING

Signs of impending misfortune were regularly sent by the gods, though you had to know where to look to find them ...

Eclipses, in particular, were signs of something unpleasant on the horizon. Following their failed siege of Syracuse in 413 BC, the Athenians decided to withdraw their men and ships and go home. However, they were halted by an eclipse of the moon, which Nicias, their superstitious commander, felt compelled to counteract by stopping everything and making a sacrifice to the gods. The gods were clearly not pleased, however, since the Syracusans used the delay to thwart the Athenian escape and capture or kill the entire expeditionary force.

Other bad signs included:

- A woman carrying a spindle in public
- Stumbling on the doorstep when going out
- An owl roosting on the house
- Snakes appearing in the house
- Walking over a grave
- Meeting a donkey carrying the herbs used to decorate a tombstone
- A crow appearing on the viewer's left (a crow on the right was good)
- The Athenians believed that spitting when dealing with an epileptic or mentally disturbed person averted evil
- An image of Medusa's head (Medusa being the lady with snakes for hair) was believed to have the power to attract and hold evil forces, and consequently was often painted or carved onto buildings

Medusa the Gorgon was beautiful until the goddess Athena turned her into the monster shown above.

GODS FOR ALL SEASONS

January	Janus, god of doorways and beginnings
March	Mars, god of war
April	From Aphrodite or Apru, her Etruscan equivalent
May	Maia, the good goddess (*bona dea*)
June	Juno, the great goddess
July	Julius Caesar (yes, he was a god, by order of his adopted son Augustus)
August	Augustus (because the son of a god is, naturally, a god too)

ODD GODS – TWELVE LESSER-KNOWN DEITIES

The great gods of the Greek and Roman pantheon, who lived on Mount Olympus, are well known, but they were not alone. Some more specific gods included:

Viriplaca The goddess who reconciled wives with their husbands after a quarrel

Vervactor The god who ensured a favourable first ploughing of fallow land

Vallonia As you might expect, the goddess of valleys

Terminus The god of boundary stones

Sterculinus The god of manure spreading

Rumina The goddess who protects nursing mothers

Pudicitia The goddess of chaste behaviour in maidens

Nona The goddess who, with Decima, presided over the final months of pregnancy

Mellona The goddess of bees and honey

Laverna The goddess of thieves and conmen

Genius Augusti The divine inspiration that separated emperors from mortals

Bonus Eventus The god of successful enterprises

The ancients sanctioned divination because they were convinced by the results.

CICERO, *ON DIVINATION*, 1.3

THE ABOMINABLE ONION

Priests abhor, detest and avoid the onion because it is the only plant whose nature it is to grow and propagate when the moon is waning. Besides, it is no proper food, either for those who want to practise abstinence and purge themselves, or for anyone enjoying a festival. For the former, because it causes thirst, and for the latter, because it forces tears from those who eat it.

PLUTARCH, *MORALIA*, 4.8

WHY DIOGENES CAN'T BE GUILTY OF THEFT

All things belong to the gods.
The wise are friends of the gods.
True friends share their property in common.
Diogenes is wise.

FROM THE TEACHING OF DIOGENES THE CYNIC

THE *FLAMEN DIALIS*

The *Flamen Dialis* was one of the most important priesthoods of Rome – but so many rituals and ceremonies surrounded the post that few people who were qualified for it actually wanted it. Here are some sample inconveniences:

- He was not allowed to go out without his cap of office
- He was not allowed to ride a horse
- If a person was brought into the house of the *Flamen Dialis* in any form of restraint he was to be untied at once and the fetters carried away through the skylight of the house's *atrium* or roof
- Only a free man was allowed to cut the hair of the *Flamen Dialis*
- The *Flamen Dialis* could never touch, nor mention, a goat, uncooked meat, ivy, or beans
- The marriage of the *Flamen Dialis* could only be ended by death, and if his wife died, he had to resign
- His clothes could not have any kind of fastenings
- The *Flamen Dialis* could not touch a dog

Women, whose mental weakness prevents them
from doing any serious work ….

VALERIUS MAXIMUS, *MEMORABLE DOINGS AND SAYINGS*, 9.1

Two Things You Didn't Know Water Could Do

Plato taught that gold solidified from water in rock:

Of all the substances that we have classed as fusible kinds of water, the densest is formed of the finest and most uniform particles. This is a unique kind, tinged with a glittering, yellow colour, that most precious of possessions, which is called gold, which has filtered through rocks and congealed there. PLATO, *TIMAEUS*, 59B

Rock crystal, meanwhile, was ice crystallized into stone. Pliny the Elder, in his *Natural History* (37.29), says that rock crystal spheres could be used to focus the sun's rays and burn blemishes from the skin or cauterize wounds.

ROCK POWER: THE PROPERTIES OF GEMSTONES

Emerald Soothed tired eyes, and an emerald ring helped good eyesight

Jasper Protected athletes from injury – and many athletes carried jasper for this reason

Amber Worn in beads about the neck or wrist, was regarded as a cure for sore throat and ague, and a preventive of insanity, asthma, dropsy, toothache and deafness

Jetstone Could cure hysteria and determine if someone was a virgin

However, the **onyx** exposed its wearer to lawsuits, bad dreams and demons

Love and Marriage

Vinegar is more prejudicial to women than to men, for it creates pains in the uterus. HIPPOCRATES, *ON THE TREATMENT OF ACUTE DISEASES*, 16

SEX EDUCATION FOR PARENTS

Philosophers tended to be male, but Aristotle was diligent in his reporting on the female of his species, though he appears to have relied more on hearsay than direct investigation. Like many Greek and Roman men, he believed that women had little control of their procreational urges, and needed careful watching to prevent them from going astray. Here is an example from the *The History of Animals*:

Girls of this age [early teens] are in great need of surveillance. At this time in particular they feel a natural urge to try out their developing sexual faculties. Unless they guard against any further impulse beyond that inevitable one which their bodily development itself provides, even those who completely abstain from passionate indulgence develop habits that blight their later life. Girls who give way to temptation become increasingly promiscuous (and the same is true of boys). If they are not protected from the temptations on all sides, the passages become dilated ... and besides, the memory of the pleasure associated with passion makes them yearn to try it again.
ARISTOTLE, *THE HISTORY OF ANIMALS*, 7.1

Roman wedding ceremony shown in idealized form on a sarcophagus.

GETTING ON ONE'S NERVES

The Romans believed that the nerves of the human body carried emotions as well as sensations, and that specific emotions resided in certain parts of the body (even today someone has a lily-liver, or no stomach for a fight). The heart was, of course, the seat of love, and one particularly extended nerve was believed to run from the heart to the third finger of the hand (not including the thumb). Naturally today no one believes anything of the sort – as a glance at the location of a wedding ring will show.

A LOVER'S PARTING

In the Roman marriage ceremony the groom parts the bride's hair with a spear. It was particularly felicitous for the marriage if the spear had been dipped in the blood of a dead gladiator.

WHIPPING UP ENTHUSIASM

Every February Rome played host to the *Lupercalia*, a festival of fertility that went back to the city's earliest days. Ceremonies began in the cave in which Romulus and Remus were believed to have been suckled by the wolf – a cave which archaeologists have recently unearthed beneath the Palatine Hill. In that cave several goats and a dog were sacrificed, and the blood of the dead animals then daubed on the faces of young men from the best families in Rome. Then, dressed in goatskins and carrying strips of leather, the lads would run along a route fixed by tradition. Anyone they came across during their journey was given a brief whipping with the leather strips. This caused a number of women to make sure that they were standing along the route, as the impact of these leather strips was considered certain to increase fertility.

SEXING CHICKS

The sex of an unborn child might be determined by taking a newly fertilized egg from a hen's nest, and keeping it warm against the mother's breast until it hatched. The sex and health of the chick would be paralleled by the child when born.

CHILLING EFFECT

Aristotle felt that men with small penises were more masculine, in that they were more likely to father children. He believed that semen cooled once it left the scrotum and lost more and more of its potency the further it had to travel.

APHRODISIACS

Roman	Greek
Garlic Ideally with chopped coriander leaves in white wine	**Garlic**
Rocket (Arugula)	**Lentils** Especially if cooked in saffron
Sparrows (Amorous little animals according to the Romans) – either eaten, or presented live to the amoratrix	**Beans** Also best in a spicy soup
	Artichokes
Carrots, asparagus, nettles All preferably served with pepper and spice to excite the blood	**Truffles**

A couple plight their troth in a classical wedding ceremony.

ENDING UP

A man comes up to Elithio Phoitete and complains: 'That slave you sold me a few days ago has just died.' To which Elithio replies: 'I'm astounded. All the time I had him, he never did anything of the sort.'

TRADITIONAL JOKE FROM ANCIENT GREECE

Preparing a youth for burial.

In Greece, after a corpse had been washed and prepared for burial, the water in which it was washed had to be poured away outside the house, lest the spirit of the departed remain on the premises. The Romans believed something similar – that the spirits of dead household members would haunt the house on 9, 11 and 13 May.

Elithio Phoitete was discussing with friends where he should build his tomb. Someone mentioned a particular place, but Elithio rejected the suggestion at once because the area was too unhealthy.

TRADITIONAL JOKE FROM ANCIENT GREECE

Dead men float face upward, dead women face down.

PLINY THE ELDER, *NATURAL HISTORY*, 7.202

The Final Destination

The souls of Greeks and Romans dwelt in the underworld. Most people have heard of the river Styx, across which the souls of the dead were ferried by the boatman Charon. Some souls were suspended there – for example, the evil Tantalus, who was trapped for all eternity with a pool he could not drink from and fruit he could not reach (hence 'tantalizing'). However, most souls eventually reached the river Lethe on the far side of the underworld. After drinking the water, memories of their previous life were erased.

> Deep in the hollow of a mountainside, by the cave which is
>   home to lazy Sleep,
> where Phoebus' rays can never reach, be it morning or noon
>   or night,
> dark vapours rise in the gloaming where silence
>   dwells ...
>
> Only the lazy Lethe whispers beneath the rock
> trickling low over pebbly shallows, bringing
>   gentle slumber.
> Before the cavern's mouth lush poppies
>   grow and countless herbs,
> from whose essence humid Night distills
>   her potions
> and sprinkles sleep across the darkening
>   world.
>
> OVID, *METAMORPHOSES*, 11.602 ff

Attic funeral urn.

IV

PERILOUS
PROPHECIES

Euripides: *The best prophet is the best guesser.*

PLUTARCH, *ON THE CESSATION OF ORACLES*, 40

*Commemorative stone of a sacrifice offered by
Marcus Aurelius to charm away the pestilence.*

Ask the Oracle

The Oracle of Zeus at Dodona, Greece, was even more ancient than that of Delphi (see p. 70). At this beautiful site the god spoke through the wind blowing through the trees. A trained interpreter listened and answered the questions that had been written down by those seeking guidance. Here are some of the questions that archaeologists have unearthed:

- What deity should we worship to live harmoniously as man and wife?
- Should I apply for citizenship in another city?
- Should I buy a town house or a farm?
- Will I have any more children?
- How do I cure my affliction?
- Will I retrieve the mattresses and pillows I have lost?
- Annyla is pregnant – who is the father?
- Is it a good idea to take up sheep-farming?
- Is it a good idea to go on this journey?
- What have I done to deserve this?

LORD OF ALL

There had spread over all the Orient an old and firm belief, that at that time [about AD 60] it was destined that someone coming from Judaea would rule the world. This prediction referred to the emperor of Rome [Vespasian, who came from Judaea to be emperor], but the people of Judaea took the prophecy as referring to one of their own.

SUETONIUS, *LIFE OF VESPASIAN*, 4

DEAL OR NO DEAL?

During the reign of Tarquin [the last king of Rome, who ruled 535–510 BC] the favour of a god or other divine being brought a wonderful stroke of good luck to the Roman state – and this good fortune was not a single occurrence but one which has endured through Rome's existence and has often been instrumental in averting terrible calamity.

A foreign woman came to the tyrant and offered to sell him nine books of prophecies. Tarquin baulked at the price and refused, whereupon she went away and burned three books. A little later she returned and offered to sell the remaining six for the same price. The general opinion was that the woman was a fool for asking the same price for the books when she herself had destroyed three of them. The woman went away, burned another three books and returned offering the remaining three at the now-standard price.

At this point Tarquin began to suspect that the woman was up to something and sent for his priests. The priests immediately recognized the signs that these books were a divinely inspired gift, and after lamenting the fate of six of them, told Tarquin to at all costs purchase the remaining three. The woman, having handed over the books told Tarquin to guard them carefully and was never seen again. DIONYSIUS OF HALICARNASSUS, *ROMAN ANTIQUITIES*, 4.62

These books, which became known as the Sybilline Books, were kept under guard in a temple, and were only consulted in moments of national crisis, or when the omens warned that such a crisis was imminent.

DOMITIAN AND THE SOOTHSAYERS

Suetonius recounts that the emperor Domitian had a number of run-ins with soothsayers, a breed that he instinctively distrusted:

There was nothing that disturbed [Domitian] so much as a prediction by the astrologer Ascletarion and what came of it. When this man stood trial before the emperor he admitted to using his powers to make certain predictions, so he was asked what his own end would be. When he heard that the soothsayer foresaw being torn apart by dogs, Domitian ordered him killed at once. But to show the man as a charlatan, he ordered that the funeral be conducted with the greatest care. During the funeral a powerful gust of wind tipped over the pyre, and dogs mangled the corpse. SUETONIUS, *LIFE OF DOMITIAN*, 15 ff

Domitian personally conducted the trial of a soothsayer from Germany, who, when consulted about a tremendous lightning storm, had announced that it foretold a change of rulers. Domitian condemned the prophet to death and was himself assassinated later that day, to be succeeded soon thereafter by Nerva.

Suetonius tells us that astrologers had informed the young Domitian of the last year, day and even hour of his life. Therefore Domitian was on guard against deadly danger on the fifth hour of the day in which he was killed. As the appointed time drew near, he waited in dread. Finally he was informed by his attendants that it was now the sixth hour. A relieved Domitian went to prepare for a bath only to find, first, that the attendants had lied and it was still the fifth hour, and secondly that an assassin was waiting in his rooms, right on schedule.

Statue of Domitian.

SNAKES IN A DREAM

Dreams were important to the ancients, and their correct interpretation even more so. However, as this professional dream interpreter pointed out, the same dream could have multiple interpretations:

A pregnant woman dreamt that she gave birth to a serpent. The child that she brought into the world became an excellent and famous public speaker. For a serpent has a forked tongue, which is also true of a public speaker. The woman was rich, to be sure, and wealth serves to pay the expenses of an education.

Another woman had the same dream and her child became a hierophant [a priest]. For the serpent is a sacred animal and plays a part in secret rites. In this case, the woman who had the dream was also a priest's wife.

Still yet another woman had the same dream and her child became an excellent prophet. For the serpent is sacred to Apollo, who is the most versed in prophecy. This woman was also a prophet's daughter.

A fourth woman had the same dream and her child turned out to be undisciplined and wanton, and he committed adultery with many of the women in the city. For the serpent slips through the most narrow holes and attempts to escape detection by observers. The woman was herself a rather wanton prostitute.

ARTEMIDORUS DALDIANUS, *THE INTERPRETATION OF DREAMS*, 4.67

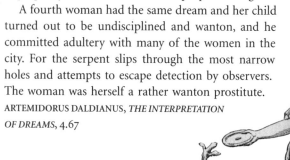

Hygieia, goddess of health, with a snake curled around her bowl. (The snake and bowl have since been adopted as a symbol by the pharmaceutical trade.)

HOROSCOPICALLY SPEAKING

Augustus, born in September, was a Libra. However, the master of Rome made much more of his rising sign (or possibly moon sign), which was Capricorn. His successor, Tiberius, born in November, was a Scorpio. The last of the Julio-Claudians, Nero, really was a Capricorn, though the biographer Suetonius assures us that Nero's horoscope was generally 'dire'.

The emperor Vespasian was told that one Mettius Pompusianus had 'an imperial horoscope'. The emperor reacted by making the man consul on the basis that the possible future emperor now owed him a big favour.

DEATH IN BABYLON

Alexander the Great and his army approached Babylon in early 323 BC. As he approached the gates, an astrologer hurried out to meet him, and warned that the king was about to make a grave error by entering the city through the eastern gate, since Alexander would enter the city facing the setting sun. Since the sun was a symbol of the Macedonian royal house, this would be an appalling omen. Alexander took his prophecies seriously, but it was now too late to march his men across marshy ground to the western gate of this huge city. In the following months the priests tried desperately with various rites to expiate the coming misfortune, but for nothing: Alexander did not leave Babylon alive.

SOME PRODIGIES

The war with Hannibal was a tense time for Rome, and the gods became unusually communicative. Some of the odd signs from 218–210 BC include:

A talking cow	**A woman** changing into a man
A rain of meat	**A lamb** born with milk in its udders
Bloodstained wheat	**Snakes** jumping out of the sea
A two-headed pig	**A pig** with a human face
A hen turning into a cock	**A baby** born with an elephant's head
Soldiers' spears spontaneously bursting into flame	

Livy's X-file
Some unidentified flying prodigies mentioned by Livy:

217 BC Ships were seen brightly visible in the heavens

217 BC Shields were seen in the sky

176 BC A burning torch was seen in the sky

100 BC A round object, like a sphere or circular shield, made its way across the sky from west to east

42 BC Something that seemed to be a weapon, or missile, rose from the earth with a great noise and flew into the sky

Some Greek prodigies

Slaughtered cattle bellowing on the spit

Unlit cauldrons coming to the boil

An eagle holding a goose

A mare giving birth to a hare

DIVINE ORDER

But who fails to observe that auspices and all other kinds of divination flourish best in the best regulated states?

CICERO, *ON DIVINATION*, 43

SIGNS AND PORTENTS

The Etymologia *of Varro says: 'The gods may show what is to come by means of defective births' (11.3.8). In fact, the word 'monster' comes from the Latin* monstrare *'to show'. Defective births had to be reported to the Roman authorities, who decided if they were messages from above.*

BORN TO RULE

One of Rome's greatest enemies, the Persian king Shapur II, reigned 70 years, from AD 309 to 379. He started his reign before his birth, when the astrologers predicted the dead king's wife would bear a son. Shapur was crowned 'in utero', with the crown being placed on his mother's belly.

A PREDICTION IN THE NICK OF TIME

When the future emperor Tiberius was at the nadir of his fortunes and in semi-exile in Rhodes he had as a confidant an astrologer called Thrasyllus, who had predicted great things for him. These prophecies had apparently failed to become reality, and Tiberius was regretting having confided in the soothsayer. Therefore Thrasyllus was invited to take a stroll by the sea with Tiberius, who had decided to test whether the soothsayer had predicted his own watery end. As they neared the sea, Thrasyllus pointed to an approaching ship and announced that it carried momentous news. Tiberius was curious enough to postpone Thrasyllus' fate, and discovered that the news was that Augustus was dead, and that he stood to inherit control of the Roman empire.

THE DELPHIC ORACLE

The Oracle of Delphi was of great antiquity, mentioned even in the poems of Homer. By the historical era in Greece few great undertakings were planned without getting the Oracle's opinion. Not everyone could get to see the Oracle, and those who did had to make a number of preliminary sacrifices and undergo purifying rituals before being allowed to put their question to the god.

That god was Apollo, to whom Delphi was sacred, and he spoke through a special priestess called the Pythia. The Pythia gave her prophecies from a chamber where she sat before a tripod, with an olive sprig in one hand. The prophecies only happened at certain times of the year, and then for relatively short periods. Beforehand the priestess would purify herself at the Castalian spring, which flows from the mountain, and burn laurel leaves and barley meal at the god's altar.

On receiving the enquiry the priestess would call out the words and visions that came to her, and the *prophetai* – those with the task of explaining the Pythia's words – would warn the enquirer that the words of the Pythia neither revealed nor hid the truth but suggested how to find it.

Some modern researchers claim that the priestess was mildly euphoric from ethylene, a sweet-smelling hydrocarbon gas that built up in her underground chamber, but her answers were always delivered calmly and clearly – these were no drug-fuelled ravings.

THE DOUBLE-EDGED SWORD

Perhaps the most famous of all the Delphic predictions was that given to Croesus of Lydia when he was contemplating an attack on the Persian empire of Cyrus. The Oracle assured Croesus that his attack would indeed destroy a great empire – though as Croesus later discovered, that empire was his own.

The Delphic Oracle. As shown here, the Pythia was screened from the sight of the enquirer.

SICKNESS FROM HEAVEN

When Spartans considered going to war with Athens in 431 BC, they naturally wanted to know how Apollo felt about it. Apollo signalled approval, even enthusiasm, for the idea, saying that if the Spartans did decide to fight he would help them. He did this in the opening years of the war by inflicting on Athens a devastating plague. The Athenians responded by upgrading their festival to Apollo at Delos, and thereafter things went better for them (for a while, at least).

SOME OTHER ORACLES

The Oracle of Zeus at Dodona in Epirus, Greece

Amun Siwa in Egypt (often consulted by Greeks)

Fortuna Primigenia at Praeneste, Italy

The Oracle of Apollo at Didyma near Miletus, western Turkey

The Sanctuary of Amphiarus at Oropus in Greece

The Oracle of Zeus Philios at Antioch in the Middle East

The Oracle at Carmel in Judaea

The Sceptics

BAH, HUMBUG!

Basically, I say, I do not give a damn for Marsian augurs, village mounte-banks, astrologers who haunt the circus grounds, or Isis-seers, or dream interpreters. APPIUS CLAUDIUS THE AUGUR. CICERO, *ON DIVINATION*, 58

THE SUPERSTITIOUS RATIONALIST

The biographer Plutarch believed in oracles, but not blindly:

Melancholy people are much subject to dreams in the night, and their dreams sometimes come true. But such people's imaginations run some-times on one thing and at other times on another. They must necessarily be right occasionally, just as people who shoot often enough must sometimes hit the target. PLUTARCH, *MORALIA*, 4.50

But elsewhere he concludes:

Let us, then, not listen to people who say that oracles are not divinely inspired. PLUTARCH, *ON THE CESSATION OF ORACLES*, 13

The 'Oracle of the Dead'

By Lake Acherousia and the river Acheron, in northwest Greece, was a portal that linked the world of the living with the realm of the dead. And on this site was built the *Necromanteion,* or 'Oracle of the Dead'. Here, according to tradition, Odysseus communicated with a dead prophet to find his way back home, and here Periander, the Tyrant of Corinth, was accused of necrophilia by the spirit of his dead wife. The site was rediscovered in the last century, but no one has yet established whether the Oracle is still in working order.

The Aquatic Chickens of Drepana

Publius Appius Claudius Pulcher was a Roman aristocrat who had a high opinion of his abilities as an admiral. Thus, when he went to take on the Carthaginians at Drepana in 249 BC, even though his fleet was poorly trained and hardly seaworthy, he insisted on attacking the enemy in their harbour.

Just before the battle, however, the priests told Claudius that the sacred chickens had failed to eat their corn – a sure warning by Jupiter of impending disaster. Claudius was unimpressed. 'If they won't eat, they can drink instead,' he replied, and ordered the chickens to be thrown overboard. Unfortunately for him, the chickens were right, and Claudius' expedition ended in the loss of 93 of his 120 ships.

In the words of Valerius Maximus: 'I don't know whether Appius Claudius was a greater disgrace to his religion or his country, seeing that he neglected the time-honoured practices of the former, and lost a fine fleet of the latter.' *MEMORABLE DOINGS AND SAYINGS*, 8.1.16

Sacred chickens on this fragment from a Roman altar signify divine approval by pecking at the grain laid out for them.

I will declare to men the unfailing will of Zeus.

APOLLO, GOD OF PROPHECY IN THE
HOMERIC HYMN TO APOLLO, 131–32

A Grim Meeting

Plutarch's *Life of Brutus* relates one ghostly encounter. After he had killed Julius Caesar, Brutus was at war with Octavian, Caesar's heir. Awake one night in his tent while the rest of his army slept, he became aware of a presence nearby – looking up, he saw a ghostly apparition, tall, ghastly and silent. The stoical Roman and phantom regarded each other in silence until Brutus finally enquired: 'Who are you, and what do you want?'

'I am your evil destiny', replied the apparition, 'and we shall meet again at Philippi.'

Calmly, Brutus responded: 'Very well, I shall see you then.'

The apparition appeared as promised on the eve of the climatic battle, in which Brutus was defeated and took his own life.

Warned in a Dream

Brutus's enemy in that battle was the future emperor Augustus. Being sick at the time (his health was always frail), Augustus was inclined to sit out the first day of the battle, but was persuaded by a friend's dream to leave his tent. The dream was prophetic, for the enemy broke into the camp, and stabbed his bedding through and through before discovering he was not in it.

Failing to Take a Hint

JULIUS CAESAR

The soothsayer Spurinna famously warned Caesar: 'Beware the Ides of March.' Caesar, on his way to the Senate (and his assassination) saw the prophet and cheerfully pointed out that he was still whole and healthy, though the Ides of March had come. 'Aye', said Spurinna dolefully, 'but they have not yet gone.'

In fact, the gods allegedly gave a few other signs to suggest all was not well:

PLUTARCH
- Lights in the sky
- Crashing sounds unexpectedly in the night
- Ill-omened birds in the Forum
- A slave with a burning but uninjured hand

STRABO
- An animal sacrificed by Caesar found to have no heart
- Caesar's wife dreaming of holding her murdered husband (as a result of wife's dreams, soothsayers were consulted and agreed that omens were bad)

SUETONIUS
- Sacred horses refusing to graze
- The discovery of an ancient oracle predicting a Julian death

And finally, Artemidorus, a Greek philosopher, gave Caesar a scroll with details of the plot and urged him to read it at once (Caesar didn't).

Julius Caesar, in a somewhat idealized bust which understates his receding hairline.

USEFUL TRIPS

During the civil wars Julius Caesar took the fight to his enemies in Africa. As his invasion fleet arrived and Caesar was disembarking, he tripped and fell flat on his face. This was an appallingly bad omen, which Caesar turned to useful propaganda by grasping the earth firmly and shouting: 'Africa – I have seized you!'

Brutus, the liberator of Rome, once travelled to Delphi with the sons of Tarquin to ask about the portentous appearance of snakes in the royal home. While they were with the Oracle, one of the sons dared ask who would be next to rule in Rome. The Oracle replied: 'The one who next kisses his mother.' Only Brutus understood the true meaning of the Oracle, and as they were leaving pretended to stumble and fall. While on the ground, he kissed the earth – the mother of all – and went on to overthrow the tyrannical Tarquin and establish the Roman Republic.

Silver tetradrachm of Perseus, minted at Amphipolis or Pella, 179–168 BC.

OUT OF THE MOUTHS OF BABES AND SUCKLINGS

When Aemilius Paulus, Roman commander for the war against Perseus of Macedon, was preparing to leave Rome, he found his daughter in tears. Asking her what was wrong, she replied: 'Perseus is dead.' It turned out that the girl had adopted a puppy and given it that name. Paulus chose to believe that the gods had sent him a sign. Perseus was indeed defeated, and died a Roman captive.

Victory sacrificing the bull of the Roman Triumphs.

TWENTY-FIRST TIME LUCKY

Just before the Battle of Pydna, the decisive battle in the war against Perseus of Macedon, there was an eclipse of the moon. The Roman commander Aemilius Paulus, a devoutly religious man, immediately sacrificed to the moon as it brightened once more. He also sacrificed a heifer to Hercules. The demi-god did not return the favourable omen that Paulus wanted, so he sacrificed another. And another. And another. (It was a Roman habit to keep sacrificing until the gods gave the sign they wanted.) Hercules held out for the first 20 heifers, but cracked on the 21st. By then Paulus had also sweetened his offer by adding the promise of dedicatory games, and a hecatomb (a sacrifice of a further 100 cattle) on account, deliverable if the Romans won. They did.

SIGNS OF GREATNESS

Signs by which leaders were discovered in Greece and Rome:

Tarquin the Elder was coming to Rome for the first time when an eagle snatched off his hat, and then brought it back again. His wife immediately understood that he would become king.

The future emperor Vespasian was enjoying a quiet drink when a dog dropped a human hand under his chair – the hand symbolizing mastery.

A certain Publius Nigidius asked Octavius why he was late coming to the Senate. When he was told that Octavius' wife had just given birth [to the emperor Augustus], he declared, perhaps sarcastically, that the future ruler of the world had been born.

An eagle dropped into the lap of Livia, wife of emperor Augustus, a white chick with a laurel branch in its beak. The chick gave birth to a large brood of white chicks and the laurel grew into an extensive grove. This was seen as proof that Livia's family and the Augustan system would flourish.

Olympias, mother of Alexander the Great, dreamed of the thunderbolts of Zeus portending his birth.

Peisistratus, tyrant of Athens, had the most direct sign from the gods imaginable. Athena herself rode with him on the chariot as he came to Athens to seize power. (Or a six-foot-tall country lass dressed as the goddess, if we are to believe the cynical Herodotus.)

The head of a child called Servius Tullius burst into flame while he slept on, unharmed by the fire. This was a sign he was to become the sixth king of Rome.

The cockerel was associated with several Greek gods including Hermes, Asclepius, Ares and, of course, Priapus. The image of the sun in this image suggests that this cockerel was about to meet its end as a sacrifice to Phoebus Apollo, the bright god.

Terracotta plaque of a girl offering a cock and libation.

MEGISTIAS

This man was a native of Acarnania, and a seer from an ancient family. He was among the small band of heroes who fought and died resisting the Persians at Thermopylae, though he took the precaution of continuing his line by sending his son to safety. He had, we are told, foreseen his end 'by way of his art'. Since he was with 300 Spartans preparing to fight to the death against at least 50,000 Persians (and possibly twice that number), Megistias wins the Antiquity Award for predicting the obvious, as well as the more memorable tribute from the great Athenian poet Simonides:

> You see here the great Megistias' tomb
> Who slew the Medes, fresh from Spercheius' fords.
> The wise seer clearly foresaw his death,
> Yet would not forsake the Spartan cause.

HERODOTUS, *THE HISTORIES*, 7.228

V

THE GOSSIP COLUMN

Certain people in antiquity attracted speculation, rumour and gossip in much the same way that celebrities do today. Augustus, Socrates and Vespasian were not only major figures in their time, but they were also possessed of a neat turn of phrase. Here are some of the collected anecdotes associated with them.

Augustus.

AUGUSTUS

From a coldly ruthless and totally unscrupulous young man, Augustus changed into the benevolent 'father' and moral guardian of his country once he achieved supreme power. Though he continued to be mercilessly strict with his own family, he was otherwise both tolerant and easy-going, as the following stories show.

PERSONAL RELATIONS

The biographer Suetonius quotes this extract from a letter written by Mark Antony to the young Augustus:

What has come over you? Are you upset because I'm sleeping with the queen [Cleopatra]? ... Am I just beginning this, or was it nine years ago? And what about you – are you really screwing only [Livia] Drusilla? Good luck to you if when you read this letter you have not been at it with Tertulla or Terentilla or Rufilla or Salvia Titisenia, or the whole lot together. Since when did it matter where or with whom you got laid?

There came to Rome a young man who bore an amazing resemblance to Augustus. Eventually the emperor got to hear of this and asked to see the boy for himself. After studying the lad for a while, Augustus finally asked: 'Tell me, was your mother ever in Rome?' The young man denied this, but added, 'However, my father came here often.'

MACROBIUS, *SATURNALIA*, 4.20

While history does not record whether Augustus' mother was actually unfaithful, the infidelities of his daughter, Julia, were more flagrant. Despite her affairs, however, her children all bore a striking resemblance to Julia's husband, Marcus Agrippa. Asked by a friend how this came to be so, Julia replied: 'A wise captain does not let passengers aboard until the cargo is in the hold.'

Augustus and his daughter always had a rather fraught relationship. On one occasion Julia came to a dinner wearing a daringly skimpy garment. Augustus, like many with a somewhat wild youth, had become prudish with age, and looked rather cross. When he saw his daughter the next day, he was mollified to see her modestly dressed. 'Last night I dressed for my husband', explained Julia, 'and today for my father.'

Seeing a slave attending to his daughter's coiffure. Augustus asked Julia if she would rather have white hair or be bald. Julia said that white hair was preferable. 'Better tell your slave to stop plucking it out then,' Augustus told her.

When the extent of Julia's affairs became known to him, Augustus was outraged. Several of Rome's smart young set were exiled for their conduct, and Julia herself was sent to live on an isolated island where all male visitors were carefully checked before being allowed to see her. Phoebe, Julia's maid and confidante, hanged herself. When told of this, Augustus grimly replied: 'I envy Phoebe's father.'

When the population of Rome, who always had a soft spot for Julia, appealed on her behalf to Augustus for mercy, the emperor ungraciously agreed to move her from her island exile to somewhat more comfortable quarters on the mainland. 'But I pray to the gods', he told the appellants, 'that you have wives and daughters like her.'

Image of Julia as imagined in a Victorian-era woodcut.

QUICK WITS

A certain Vatinus, who had been suffering from gout, was heard to be boasting that he had recovered and that these days he could walk a mile. 'I believe it', Augustus remarked; 'The days are getting longer.' (Vatinus was not a popular man. After being pelted with stones by the public at the games, he prevailed on the magistrates to ban the spectators from hurling anything but fruit. When someone asked a jurist whether a pine cone was a fruit he was told: 'If you propose to throw it at Vatinus, it is.')

Augustus was harsh toward his daughter, but positively easy-going compared with some other rulers in the ancient world. When he heard that King Herod – the same who ordered the massacre at Bethlehem – had executed another of his children for alleged treason, Augustus exclaimed (in a sentence that translates very neatly from Latin): 'I'd rather be one of Herod's goats than one of his kids.'

When a certain Vettius ploughed up a field that included a memorial to his father, Augustus remarked: 'This is indeed cultivating your father's memory.' (Another joke that works perfectly in translation.)

When Augustus went to the races at the Circus Maximus, he came across a man who had brought a packed lunch with him. Annoyed at the man's apparent idleness, the emperor pointed out: 'Even I go home when I want to eat.' Not in the least intimidated, the subject of imperial disapproval replied: 'Well, no one's going to steal your place, are they?'

Augustus once ordered a presumptuous young soldier to be dismissed from his service. The unfortunate man pleaded for a second chance. 'How can I go home after this?' he demanded. 'What can I tell my father?' The emperor replied: 'Tell him that you didn't find me to your satisfaction.'

One Vedius Pollio invited Augustus to dine by his fishpond, which was stocked with large lampreys. When a slave infuriated Pollio by breaking a crystal cup, Pollio ordered the slave to be thrown to the lampreys. The slave fled to Augustus begging to be killed in some other way than by the blood-sucking fish. The emperor pardoned the slave and ordered Pollio to show him the rest of his cups. Augustus then ordered them smashed, and the fishpond to be filled in.

A petitioner was offering his scroll to the emperor, but was too scared to approach him closely. Augustus told the man: 'You are not offering a penny to an elephant, you know.'

On his return from the Battle of Actium, Augustus was met by a man who presented him with a crow trained to squawk: 'Hail Caesar! Victorious general!' A delighted Augustus richly rewarded the man for his loyal support, as he was not particularly popular in Italy at this time. Later Augustus learnt that the man had a colleague who had trained another crow to give a similar greeting to Antony, in case Augustus was defeated by his rival. An amused Augustus simply ordered the two rogues to split his gift between them.

Augustus was invited to a dinner, and found that his host had made no great preparations for entertaining the emperor. Rather than comment on the rather ordinary fare, Augustus simply murmured to his host as he was leaving: 'I had no idea I was so good a friend of yours.'

On the day he died, Augustus ordered his hair to be combed, and his sunken cheeks adjusted before he saw his friends for the last time. He asked them: 'So have I played my part well in this little drama?' and added:

> If I've done well, give loud applause,
> shouts of joy in this actor's cause.

This was the traditional parting couplet of an actor as he left the stage for the final time.

SOCRATES

One of the greatest citizens of ancient Athens, Socrates (469–399 BC) was not greatly appreciated by all during his lifetime. He baffled and angered many of those who had dealings with him, and though both wise and gentle, and attracting the passionate devotion of men like Alcibiades and Plato, he was also both stubborn and heroically contrary. The true marvel is that the usually intolerant Athenians put up with this extraordinary 'gadfly' for as long as they did.

THE 'WISEST MAN ALIVE'

The Oracle at Delphi once announced that no one was wiser than Socrates. On hearing this, Socrates took the trouble to meet and converse with the great, good and wise of Athens. Afterwards he announced that the Oracle was correct, for though he knew nothing, unlike the others he had conversed with, he was aware of the fact. This made him wiser than them.

Because Socrates accepted no money for his teaching, he was never well off. A friend was therefore surprised to see him carefully examin-

ing some of the more luxurious wares on display in the Agora. Since Socrates hardly ever purchased anything, the friend asked why he came to the market so regularly. Socrates replied: 'Because I am always astonished to see the number of things that I don't actually need.'

Socrates, probably the wisest, but certainly not the prettiest, man in Athens.

---

*Often while raising points of argument or in discussion people got
violent with him, and he was jostled, shoved about and laughed at.
He took all this patiently. Once, after some particularly rough
handling, someone asked him why he did nothing about it.
[In response] Socrates asked: 'If I were kicked by a donkey,
would you want me to prosecute that as well?'*

DIOGENES LAËRTIUS, *LIFE OF SOCRATES*, 6

Xenophon's admiration for Socrates might be traced back to a report that Socrates saved Xenophon's life when the latter had fallen from his horse during a battle against the Thebans. After the rest of the Athenians had fled, Socrates retreated slowly, turning viciously on anyone who attacked him. Socrates also saved the life of the aristocrat Alcibiades in the Battle of Potidaea, for which the young man afterwards gave him fulsome praise.

Alcibiades later offered Socrates a substantial plot of land on which to build himself a house. Socrates refused, saying: 'If it seemed I needed shoes, and you gave me a piece of leather to make myself shoes with, I'd be laughed at if I took it.'

SOCRATES AND XANTHIPPE

On one occasion Socrates' wife Xanthippe was upset because friends were coming for dinner and all she could afford was very basic food. Socrates replied: 'If they are true friends they will understand. If they aren't, their opinions don't matter anyway.'

A man once asked Socrates if he should marry. He replied: 'Whether you do so or not, you will regret it.' His own marriage was stormy, which later caused him to change his opinion to: 'Every man should marry. His wife will either make him happy or make him a philosopher.'

Xanthippe on one occasion first screamed at Socrates, and then threw water over him. Socrates remarked: 'Did I not say that Xanthippe was thundering now, and after that I'd get rain?'

———•••———

Socrates often remarked ... 'Just as when a horseman has learned to manage a restive horse he can easily cope with all the others, if I can live with Xanthippe, I can get along with almost anyone else.'

DIOGENES LAËRTIUS, *LIFE OF SOCRATES*, 17

———•••———

When Alcibiades told him he should not put up with such abuse from Xanthippe, Socrates said his wife was simply background noise: 'I'm as used to it as sailors are to the sound or rope and pulley – and you yourself [being a landowner] hear geese cackling on your premises all the time.' Alcibiades answered: 'Yes, but the geese produce eggs and goslings.' 'So', said Socrates, 'so much more should I tolerate Xanthippe, who brings me children.'

Socrates versus Athens

———•••———

In 406 BC Socrates was an official of the Athenian assembly when eight admirals were charged with misconduct. Athenian law said that no one could be condemned to death collectively – each had to have his own trial. However, the assembly, whipped up by enemies of the admirals, was insisting that the six men present be condemned collectively (two admirals had very sensibly refused to return to Athens and had to be condemned *in absentia*). Socrates used the authority of his office to prevent this, though the assemblymen threatened him with fines, impeachment and then imprisonment. Yet, Socrates remained adamant, and finally the assembly had to wait until the next day – when Socrates was no longer in office – before its members could get on with their legalized lynching. (Which they later regretted, claiming demagogues had led them astray.)

On another occasion, after a *coup d'état* in Athens, Socrates was ordered to bring a man from his home to face execution. Socrates politely but firmly refused. Happily, a counter-revolution saved the philosopher from execution.

Melitus, the son of Melitus of Pittea, impeaches Socrates, the son of Sophroniscus, of Alopece. Socrates is guilty, in that he does not believe in the gods whom the city worships, but introduces other strange deities. He is guilty, too, of corrupting the young men, and the punishment this carries is death.

THE EXACT CHARGE AGAINST SOCRATES, AS RECORDED BY
THE HISTORIAN FAVORINUS FROM THE WORDING OF AN
INSCRIPTION IN THE TEMPLE OF CYBELE.

When Socrates was told he was to face charges of corrupting the young men of the city, he simply continued to conduct his philosophical discussions as before. A friend of Socrates came across him discussing every topic but his impending trial, and put it to the philosopher that he might better spend his time preparing his argument to the jury. Socrates turned to him and said: 'What? Do you think that I have not spent my entire life preparing my defence?'

Men of Athens, my prosecutors have told you to be on your guard against being deceived by my eloquence, yet their own words have been so persuasive that I hardly know who I am any more.

SOCRATES OPENS HIS DEFENCE WHILE ON TRIAL FOR HIS LIFE.
PLATO, *APOLOGY OF SOCRATES*, 1.1

Once the jury had found Socrates guilty, the defence and prosecution were required to give alternative sentences for the jury to choose between. The prosecution demanded the death sentence. Socrates said that for his part, he thought he deserved to be sentenced to a pension and free meals from the state.

As he was awaiting his fatal dose of hemlock, one of Socrates' supporters told him: 'It is hard to bear, seeing you put to death so unjustly.' Socrates serenely enquired: 'Would you be any happier if they had a good reason?'

ARISTOPHANES

Among Socrates' many admirers wasn't Aristophanes, the leading satirical playwright of Athens. He dedicated an entire play – *The Clouds* – to lampooning the philosopher and his works. (Interestingly, the play was his least successful on the Athenian stage.) Socrates took it calmly, remarking that those comments that were accurate gave him a chance to recognize faults in himself, and those comments that were rubbish, were rubbish, and could be cast aside.

VESPASIAN

Rome's ninth emperor (AD 69–79) was a total contrast to the highly bred and glamorous Julio-Claudians. He was tolerant, practical and pragmatic, and did a great job of getting the empire back on its feet after Nero had ruined its finances. This gave him a well-deserved reputation as a penny-pincher – something that was probably also a reaction to financial difficulties when he was younger. The anecdotes here come entirely from Suetonius' *Life of Vespasian*, which captures perfectly the mixture of bathos and earthy fun that Vespasian brought to the job.

EARLY CAREER

For a long time Vespasian made no attempt to add a senator's purple stripe to his toga, though his brother quickly gained one. Eventually Vespasian's mother persuaded him to add it by constantly referring to him as his brother's *anteambulo* (the person who walked before a patron to clear the way). *LIFE OF VESPASIAN*, 2

When Vespasian became a candidate for the aedileship, he won the office only after one failure and then just scraping into sixth place (out of six). As well as licensing bars and brothels, one of the duties of an aedile was to keep the roads clean. Vespasian proved so bad at the latter task that Caligula, 'furious at his dereliction of duty in failing to keep the streets clean, ordered him to be covered with muck [from the street], which the soldiers accordingly shovelled into his purple-striped toga.' *LIFE OF VESPASIAN*, 5

Financial difficulties led to Vespasian mortgaging all his landholdings to his brother. He gained the nickname of 'the Muleteer' because he became a second-hand mule dealer to keep afloat financially. His first office as governor in Africa was a job he performed with distinction, 'apart from that riot at Hadrumetum, where he was pelted with turnips.' *LIFE OF VESPASIAN*, 4

Vespasian temporarily joined the imperial entourage of Nero, but soon fell out of favour due to his inability to appreciate the emperor's artistic performances. 'He bitterly offended Nero by either leaving while the emperor was in full song, or, when he stayed, by falling asleep.' *LIFE OF VESPASIAN*, 4

Vespasian.

AS EMPEROR

When a young man came to thank Vespasian for being given a [military] commission, Vespasian recoiled in disgust at the reek of perfume on the man. He revoked the appointment on the spot, commenting: 'I would rather you smelled of garlic.'

LIFE OF VESPASIAN, 8

Senators should not have to suffer abuse or foul language, but it is a proper and lawful response if the senator uses it first.

IMPERIAL RULING ON A CONTRETEMPS BETWEEN A SENATOR AND AN ORDINARY CITIZEN. *LIFE OF VESPASIAN*, 9

When some flatterers made an attempt to trace the origin of his family to the founders of [the city of] Reate and a companion of Hercules whose tomb still stands on the Via Salaria, the proudly non-pedigreed Vespasian laughed in their faces.

LIFE OF VESPASIAN, 12

Vespasian banished the cynic philosopher Demetrius. He met the man when he was himself outside Rome and Demetrius not only failed to stand and salute him, but snarled some insult or the other. Vespasian merely responded with the reprimand 'Bad dog!' [Cynics originally got their name from kynos, *which is Greek for 'dog'.]*

LIFE OF VESPASIAN, 13

Striding along and waving a lance that casts a long shadow ...

VESPASIAN QUOTES HOMER'S *ILIAD* (7.213) ON SEEING A TALL, NAKED AND VERY WELL-ENDOWED MAN

A mechanical engineer came up with the means to transport some heavy columns to the Capitol. Vespasian richly rewarded the man for his invention, but refused to use it, saying: 'I've got the working classes to feed.'

LIFE OF VESPASIAN, 18

Vespasian's expression [as surviving statues show] was always somewhat strained. When a performer was making witty comments about members of his audience, Vespasian challenged the humorist to make a joke about him too. The reply came zinging back: 'Certainly, as soon as you have finished relieving yourself!'

LIFE OF VESPASIAN, 20

He bedded a woman who informed him that she was dying of love for him. Afterwards he rewarded her efforts with 400,000 sesterces. When his bookkeeper asked how he wanted the item entered in his accounts, he replied: 'To passion for Vespasian.'

LIFE OF VESPASIAN, 22

THE IMPERIAL SKINFLINT

One of Vespasian's attendants asked for a favour for his brother. The emperor made enquiries and found that this was no brother but someone who had bribed the attendant to ask for the favour. Vespasian granted the favour on being paid the same bribe. He then told his attendant: 'You need to find another brother – the one you thought you had turns out to be mine.' *LIFE OF VESPASIAN, 23*

His son Titus complained it was unbecoming of an emperor to charge a tax on public urinals. In reply Vespasian picked up a coin and held it under his son's nose. 'Does that smell bad to you?' he asked. (Until recently public urinals in Paris were still called *vespasiennes*.)

[Vespasian] blatantly sold posts to candidates and acquittals to men facing prosecution, whether the latter were innocent or guilty. Some believed he even deliberately promoted his most rapacious officials to higher posts. That way they were even richer when he later condemned them [and confiscated their ill-gotten gains]. Such men were commonly called his 'sponges', as he let them soak up the money that he squeezed out of them later.

LIFE OF VESPASIAN, 16

When the sailors of the fleet complained that regular marches from Ostia and Puteoli to Rome were wearing down the hobnails on their boots, and asked for an allowance for the replacement costs, Vespasian ordered that in future they should march barefoot.

LIFE OF VESPASIAN, 8

LAST DAYS

As it was customary for emperors to be deified by the Senate on their death, when Vespasian realized he was mortally ill he remarked: 'It's not looking good. I think I'm turning into a god.' LIFE OF VESPASIAN, 23

When a violent attack of diarrhoea almost made him pass out, Vespasian struggled to get to his feet, saying, 'An emperor ought to die standing,' and died in the arms of those who tried to help him up.

LIFE OF VESPASIAN, 24

It was customary at funerals for an actor to wear a mask of the deceased and to behave in a similar manner. For Vespasian an actor called Favour was chosen. In keeping with the imperial character, he asked the organizers in a loud voice how much his funeral procession was costing. When told 'Ten million sesterces', he cried out, adding: 'Give me a hundred thousand and throw me into the Tiber.'

LIFE OF VESPASIAN, 19

VI

OF LOVE & LADIES

In a relentlessly patriarchal, and more than somewhat misogynistic world, the women of antiquity were meant to accept that their menfolk knew best. Here are a few who were bucking the trend thousands of years before anyone had heard of feminism.

———

Drawing of a couple from a sepulchre in the Louvre.

SILPHIUM, THE PLANT OF LOVE

Women across the ancient world had reason to be grateful to silphium, a rare plant that grew only around the town of Cyrene in North Africa. For as well as being used in Greek and Roman cookery, and as a medicine against coughs, fevers and indigestion, it was also taken as a birth-control measure (and in larger doses possibly even stimulated the body into abortion). Modern scientists have speculated that the plant contained naturally high levels of a chemical resembling oestrogen, which is still used in oral contraceptives today.

In a world where pregnancy was often fatal for the mother (the daughter of Julius Caesar, for example, died after a difficult childbirth, as did Cicero's daughter Tullia), silphium offered an alternative to both a risky birth and the brutal necessity of killing a child that the family was unable to feed. Little wonder that it was considered to be worth its weight in gold.

The mainstay of the Cyrene economy, the plant became extinct in the first century AD, possibly as a result of the steady desertification of North Africa and overgrazing (the meat of animals fed on silphium was meant to be particularly delicious).

It is possible that one remnant of this extraordinary plant remains in modern culture. It is often remarked that the heart used to symbolize romance looks very little like the actual human organ. However, it does look *exactly* like pictures of silphium seed.

SAPPHO, LYRIC POET

We know two things for certain about Sappho. The first is that she was a Lesbian – in that she came from the island of Lesbos in the Aegean Sea. The other is that she was a superb lyric poet – so good that later admirers called her the last of the Muses. Apart from these two details, almost everything else written about this unusual woman is speculation, conjecture and sometimes highly overheated fantasy.

In her writing, Sappho tells us she had a brother and a daughter: 'I have a child, my darling Cleis, beautiful as golden flowers.' These family members could be as real or unreal as the young ladies who feature in many of her yearning verses.

Greece in 650 BC was radically remote from the present era, and the details of how women lived are so sketchy that it is hard today to establish how far Sappho was able to translate the powerful eroticism of her writing into practical accomplishment. It is worth noting that ancient tradition attributed Sappho with an impressive string of male lovers, and the idea that she was purely attracted to women only later developed in medieval Europe. In fact, Greek legend has Sappho leaping off a cliff to her death after failing to win the love of a beautiful young ferryman called Phaeon.

Here Sappho speaks on her own behalf – first from her only complete poem to survive the last two-and-a-half millennia.

> If now she flees, soon she shall follow
> She spurns gifts – but will offer them tomorrow
> If she knows not love, she will feel it still
> However much against her will
>
> *PRAYER TO APHRODITE*, VERSE 6
>
> The moon has set, and the Pleiades; the midnight's gone,
>   time is passing. And I lie alone.
>
> FRAGMENT 48

Roman scribesses.

Is he a god that he can sit so in your presence,
Hearing your sweet voice and lovely laughter so close to him?
(That voice which makes my heart race so in my chest)
For I can hardly speak when I see you
My tongue is useless, my eyes are blind, and my ears ring
And a subtle fire races beneath my skin.

FRAGMENT 2

Verses such as these were called lyric, as they were meant to be sung to a lyre. More of her poetry is constantly emerging, some from papyri found under desert sands, and once, memorably, on cloth used to wrap a mummy. Perhaps eventually enough will be found to recreate the famous nine books that made up the body of her work.

LOVE BITES

Elithio wandered into the bedroom of his grandmother while drunk and climbed into bed with her. His outraged father followed him in and immediately began beating the living daylights out of him. 'Okay, fair enough', said Elithio. 'I deserve it for getting into your mother's bed. But you've been getting into my *mother's bed for years, and I've never said a word.'*

TRADITIONAL JOKE FROM ANCIENT GREECE

It's my bloody birthday, and I've got to spend it in the dreary countryside without my Cerinthus! What's better than being in the city?

PROTEST BY SULPICIA, TEENAGE POET, FIRST CENTURY AD

CARPE DIEM WITH CATULLUS

Let us live, my Lesbia, and let us love,
and let the words of the aged, and ever so proper,
be worth less than nothing to us.
The sun may set and rise again:
but when our short day is done,
we'll sleep for an everlasting night.
So give now a thousand kisses …

CATULLUS TO HIS LOVE, *CARMINA*, 5

'Lesbia' is believed to have been Clodia, an aristocratic woman who scandalized Rome with her wild lifestyle in the last days of the Roman Republic. The poet Catullus (87–57 BC) fell head over heels for her – a close ancestor of the later emperor Claudius – and was heartbroken when she casually broke off their relationship. After his disillusionment, some of his later verses about her were brutally pornographic.

A DIALOGUE IN GRAFFITI

Comment 1: *Successus the weaver loves Iris, the barkeeper's slave girl. Even though she does not love him, he begs her to have pity.*
Comment 2: *Get lost.*
Comment 3: *Why are you getting in my way, Mr Jealousy? Give way to a handsomer man. I'm better looking and being wronged here.*
Comment 4: *I've spoken. What I have written is all there is to say. You might love Iris. She doesn't love you.*

A DRAMA ENACTED ON THE WALLS OF THE BAR OF PRIMA IN POMPEII, CIL 4.8258 **ff**

TILL DEATH DO US PART

Lycoris has buried all the female friends she had. If only she were friends with my wife!

MARTIAL, *EPIGRAMS*, 4.24

WOMEN WHO LED ARMIES IN ANTIQUITY

Fulvia The wife of Mark Antony and leader of a rebellion against Octavian (later Augustus). She was finally killed in a siege at Perusia (modern-day Perugia) in Italy in 40 BC.

Zenobia Queen of Palmyra, defeated by the emperor Aurelian in AD 273.

Cleopatra of Egypt Who is often, and probably wrongly, supposed to have lost the Battle of Actium for Mark Antony in 32 BC.

Artemisia of Caria Whose heroism in battle in 480 BC caused Xerxes, the Persian King of Kings, to remark: 'My men are women and my women men.'

Mavia Queen of the Saracens, led a revolt against the Romans in AD 378.

NOMINA ANTIQUAE

Women's names still used today:

Roman	**Greek**
Aemilia, Livia, Drusilla, Cornelia, Octavia, Julia, Antonia, Camilla, Silvia, Vivian(a)	Helen, Hermione, Agatha, Alexa, Corinna, Eunice, Irene, Melissa, Theodora

BEFORE MOUTHWASH

A man with bad breath asked his wife: 'Why do you hate me?'
To which she replied: 'Because you make love to me.'

TRADITIONAL JOKE FROM ANCIENT GREECE

THE LOVE LIFE OF JULIUS CAESAR

Wives (in succession): Cornelia, Pompeia, Calpurnia.

A young man once broke into Pompeia's house allegedly to seduce her. Although Pompeia knew nothing until afterwards, Caesar divorced her because 'Caesar's wife must be above suspicion.'

Lovers: Cleopatra of Egypt; Servilia, mother of Brutus; Servilia's daughter, Tertia; Eunoë, queen of Mauritania; Nicomedes, king of Bithynia.

King Nicomedes is a controversial case. Caesar always denied it, though his enemies were fond of calling him the 'queen of Bithynia', and when Caesar was once in the Senate listing gifts that Nicomedes had given him, Cicero remarked: 'We all know what you got from him, and what you gave.'

Head of a woman from a marble bust found on the Acropolis.

SPARTAN MOTHERS

For those who wonder how Spartan mothers felt about their newborn sons being exposed on Mount Taygetos to see whether they were tough enough, we need only consider the following comment:
'So take a step closer.'

SPARTAN MOTHER TO A SON WHO HAD COMPLAINED HIS SWORD WAS TOO SHORT

Epitaph for Erotion,
a Slave Girl Aged 6

Now let her frolic again with her old companions
Chatter, and once more lisp my name.
And let the soft grass lie over her fragile bones:
Lie lightly on her, Earth, she was never heavy on you.

MARTIAL, *EPIGRAMS*, 5.34

With his usual appalling cynicism Martial later reused this last touching couplet in *Epigrams*, 9.29 to bid farewell to someone he disliked:

May the earth be light upon you ...
So that the dogs can more easily dig you up.

Diners enjoy some post-prandial relaxation.

LIQUID SEDUCTION

*The table laid offers a chance for more than just a feast
If you look close, you can find something to go with the wine
Often rosy Eros has held tight to Bacchus,
Drawing him close with soft arms
And when wine soaks Cupid's tipsy wings,
He stays a captive of the place.*

OVID, *THE ART OF LOVE*, 1.7

THE WAY TO A WOMAN'S HEART ...

Since nothing charms the opposite sex like a well-cooked dish, we offer modern seducers and seductresses this Roman meal in three courses, adapted from the cookbook of Apicius. Roman recipes were aides-memoires for experienced chefs and seldom included quantities or cooking times, so cautious experimentation is required.

ENTRÉE

A SMALL FISH DISH

several filleted and boiled small
   fishes or whole small sardines
1 handful of dried grapes
1 large pinch of freshly ground
   pepper
1 large pinch of oregano
1 spoonful of ground levisticum
   root
2 small onions, diced
½ wineglass of oil
1 dash of liquamen (see p. 138 –
   use sea salt if liquamen is not
   available)

Mix the ingredients (apart from the fish) together and put in a casserole dish. Cook until done. Stir in the fish. Thicken the mix with flour and serve.

MAIN COURSES

BRAIN PUDDING

1 spoonful of peppercorns
several stalks of lovage (use
   parsley if lovage is not available)
1 dollop of oregano
1 cooked brain of sheep or calf
5 eggs
mushrooms (for serving)
soup

Grind the pepper, lovage and oregano with a mortar and pestle, moisten with soup then add the brains and mix until smooth and lump-free. Add the eggs and continue mixing well, occasionally thinning out the mixture with soup. Spread the mixture on a metal pan and cook in the oven. When cooked, unload it onto a clean table, and cut to size. Now prepare a sauce, again using pepper, lovage and oregano. Boil, thicken with flour and strain. Heat the brain pudding in this sauce thoroughly, and serve with pepper and mushrooms.

OR, ROAST WILD BOAR

1 wild boar (use pork chops if
  boar not available)
1 handful of cumin
peppercorns
salt
honey
wine
retsina

If not yet dead, kill your boar, and clean it by removing intestines, etc. Cover liberally with salt and crushed cumin and leave to drain overnight. Season with crushed peppercorns, and then bake whole in oven. Meanwhile reduce the wine in a saucepan, and make into a broth by adding honey and retsina. Thicken with flour as required and pour over the cooked boar. Serve with seasonal vegetables.

ROSE WINE

rose petals
honey
wine according to taste
(white from Picenum is
  recommended)

Get a small linen bag, and add freshly plucked rose petals (use only the red part – the lower white part should be removed). Soak in the wine for seven days. After this time, remove the sack and replace the petals. Repeat this for one more week. Add honey for sweetening, and a few hours later drain the wine through a sieve. Experiment to see how many petals to add, noting that too many can be a powerful emetic (which, depending on the outcome of the above recipes, may be no bad thing).

SPICY DESSERT

peppercorns (vary amount
  to taste)
nuts
honey
rue
retsina
3 eggs
milk

Crush the pepper and nuts (reserving some of the nuts), then add most of the honey and all of the rue, retsina, milk and eggs. Mix well. Bake the mixture, and then pour the remaining honey over and sprinkle with the reserved crushed nuts.

WILD AND WICKED WOMEN
(WHO SPENT LITTLE TIME IN THE KITCHEN)

TWO WIVES OF CLAUDIUS

MESSALINA

While the emperor Claudius was conquering Britain, his nymphomaniac wife Messalina sought other conquests. In a 'duel' she allegedly challenged one of Rome's top prostitutes and (according to Pliny the Elder) won by entertaining 25 clients in quick succession.

This august harlot was shameless enough to prefer a common mat to the imperial couch ... she took her place in a brothel reeking with overused bed-covers. Entering an empty cell reserved for herself under the feigned name of Lycisca, her nipples bare and gilded and exposed ... Here she graciously received all comers, asking from each his fee; and when at length the keeper dismissed his girls, she remained to the very last before closing her cell, and with passion still raging hot within her, went sorrowfully away.
JUVENAL, *SATIRES*, VI

Perhaps much of Messalina's reputation was from scandalous rumour, but Messalina certainly over-reached herself by 'divorcing' Claudius and taking a younger lover in a highly public marriage. She was forced to commit suicide.

Left *Messalina.* Opposite *Agrippina Minor.*
For most of the time Messalina was married to Claudius, Agrippina was in exile, a fact which protected her from Messalina's jealousy and probably saved her life.

AGRIPPINA MINOR

Agrippina, Claudius' next wife, could plead difficult family circumstances in her defence – she had Caligula as a brother and Nero as a son.

Caligula exiled Agrippina for treason and infidelity, and for a while the great-granddaughter of the emperor Augustus made her living diving for sponges. When Caligula died, she returned to favour and married Claudius, though as she was his niece Roman incest laws had to be modified to make this possible.

Agrippina was popular with the Roman people, and for a while her support was essential to Claudius' failing regime. When this support became less necessary and he appeared to be contemplating a change of wives, Claudius ate a dish of mysteriously poisoned mushrooms and died. Agrippina's son, the tyrannical and monumentally incompetent Nero, inherited the empire.

Possibly because she tried too hard to restrain her wayward child, Agrippina fell from favour, though it was reported she tried everything (including attempts at incestuous seduction) to win Nero back. Eventually, fearing that she would ally against him with Claudius' own son, Britannicus, Nero decided to kill his mother.

After a pretended reconciliation at a coastal resort, he sent his mother home in a boat with a cabin designed to collapse and crush those inside. Agrippina survived, whereupon the desperate sailors tried to drown her by sinking the boat. This was unlikely to work on a former sponge diver, so Nero abandoned subtlety and sent soldiers with orders to do the deed directly.

When she saw the swords, Agrippina bitterly told the executioners: 'Aim the first blow at my womb.'

OLYMPIAS, THE SNAKE QUEEN

Olympias, the mother of Alexander the Great, was a member of a snake-worshipping cult of the god Dionysus. She often had snakes about her person, and even slept with them in her bed. Originally a princess from the kingdom of Epirus in western Greece, she soon rose to prominence as the foremost of the wives of Philip II of Macedon. (Philip generally kept six or seven spares as well as his main wife.)

Olympias and Philip had a turbulent marriage, with Olympias storming home to her father on occasion and allegedly taking lovers. Indeed, on one occasion when she was particularly cross with Philip, she claimed that it was not the king but Zeus himself who had impregnated her with Alexander.

When Philip was assassinated, Olympias made sure that the assassin of her husband received a magnificent tomb, and she ordered the sword with which the deed was done to be given a place of honour at a temple in Delphi. Olympias also took advantage of Philip's death to conduct a mini-purge of the family, killing some of Philip's offspring, and forcing others to commit suicide.

After Alexander's death, Olympias remained active and lethal in politics and caused several more rivals to die in cruel and ingenious ways. She was finally brought down by her enemy Cassander, after a siege at Pydna. After surrendering she was killed without a trial and her remains were left unburied.

*Gold medallion
of Olympias.*

TWO *HETERÆ* OF GREECE:
PHRYNE AND LAÏS

It's a woman's skill, to strip wealth from an ardent lover.
OVID, *THE ART OF LOVE*, 1.11

A youth offers cash to a woman holding a mirror.

The exact status of *heterae* – 'companions' – has been the source of argument for centuries. Once they were considered courtesans, almost parallel with the geishas of Japan, but a revisionist argument claims that they were essentially prostitutes and, like most ancient women, victims of a brutal patriarchal ethos. *Heterae* like Phryne and Laïs may have begged to differ.

Phryne lived in the fourth century BC and famously charged her clients according to how she felt about them. She shared her bed with the philosopher Diogenes of Sinope without a fee (because she only wanted him for his mind), but set the tariff for an ugly king from Asia Minor so high that he had to increase taxes in his kingdom. Phryne is believed to have been the model for the sculptor Praxiteles' famous Aphrodite of Cnidos (on which the Venus de Milo is based).

Oddly enough this famous beauty was called 'toad' (which is the literal translation of *phryne*) – perhaps due to her yellowish complexion.

Phryne was usually modestly dressed. At the great assembly of the Eleusinia and at the festival of Poseidon, when crowds gathered for the occasion, she only took off her cloak before going for a swim. That was enough for a painter called Apelles, who portrayed her leaving the water as Aphrodite rising from the sea, a theme echoed by the artist Botticelli (who used a different and nuder model).

Her lifestyle caused Phryne to be brought before the Areopagus (the local magistrates). Her lawyer – who was paid in kind – famously removed her garments and asked who could condemn one who was so evidently 'Aphrodite's handmaiden'. (It should be remembered that in the ancient world, exceptional beauty was a sign of divine favour.)

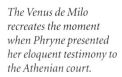

The prosecutor, one Euthias, was so outraged by the subsequent 'not guilty' verdict that he never brought another case before the court.

In later life, Phryne became fabulously wealthy. When the walls of Thebes were thrown down by Alexander the Great, she offered to pay for the rebuilding if the Thebans would agree to the inscription: 'What Alexander overthrew, Phryne restored.'

The Venus de Milo recreates the moment when Phryne presented her eloquent testimony to the Athenian court.

Laïs was apparently a beautiful lass from Sicily who was sold as a slave in Corinth. Her beauty was matched by her wit and charm, and she had no difficulty in obtaining her freedom. She had a reputation for capriciousness that was matched only by her massive fee, which rumour set at 10,000 drachmas – about what a hard-working labourer earned in a lifetime. It was allegedly such fees that inspired the Greek proverb: 'Not everyone can [afford to] visit Corinth.'

Laïs fell in love with a handsome young victor of the Olympic Games, who promised to take her away to Cyrene. (In fact the ungentlemanly athlete kept his word by sailing off with her portrait.)

In old age, she became something of an alcoholic, and was buried in a splendid tomb – Corinth was by then very proud of her – with a sculpture that depicted a lioness tearing at a ram.

The many stories told of Laïs are often conflated with another young woman of the same name (who was probably the one born in Sicily), to the extent that it is now impossible to say which Laïs was which. In one such story the famous orator Demosthenes wanted to enjoy the favours of the woman whose beauty was the wonder of Greece. When told of the huge fee, Demosthenes abandoned his quest saying: 'That's too much to pay for something I would have regretted anyway.'

It was certainly the younger Laïs who died gruesomely in Thessaly, where the local ladies took exception to her presence and stoned her to death. Plutarch tells us that an indignant Aphrodite consequently inflicted the population with a pestilence that only abated when the repentant people dedicated a temple to love.

> I am Laïs who laughed exultant over Greece,
> Who gave young lovers great delight.
> Now aged, I yield my mirror to Aphrodite.
> What I now am I do not wish to see,
> Since what I was I cannot be.

PLUTARCH, *GREEK ANTHOLOGY*, 71

VII

BEASTLY
TALES

To the ancients, animals were either exotic or threatening, beasts of burden or treasured friends. And, of course, meals with legs. A Roman could admire the beauty of birdsong in the morning and eat the singer that evening without noting any contradiction in his actions.

*Head of a horse from the eastern gable
of the Parthenon.*

HANNIBAL THE SNAKE BOMBER

Hannibal was inferior in ships, and was no match for his enemy in force. Therefore he ordered as many poisonous snakes as possible to be brought together alive, and to be put into clay pots, of which he had collected a large number. He then ordered all his captains to attack the ship of King Eumenes [the enemy commander], and to be content with simply defending themselves against others, as they might easily do with the aid of the vast number of serpents. ... When these were thrown onto the enemy ships, the soldiers laughed at them because they couldn't understand why it had been done. But once they had their ships filled with snakes, they couldn't deal with snakes and Hannibal together, so they retreated. CORNELIUS NEPOS, *THE GREAT COMMANDERS: HANNIBAL*, 10–11

THE ORACULAR SNAKE OF ALEXANDER OF ABONOTEICHUS

The diviner and fortune-teller Alexander of Abonoteichus flourished in the early years of the second century AD. He pronounced on matters of health and relationships, mixed with predictions, delivering his inspired messages by way of a huge snake that lay wrapped around his neck as he spoke.

This snake was worth well over its weight in gold, since in a single year it is said to have assisted Alexander in giving over 80,000 pronouncements at just over a drachma each (this at a time when 500 drachmas would keep a family for a year).

PETS

Despite killing beasts with great enthusiasm in the arena, many Romans were fond of animals. All of the following were kept by the Romans as pets: dogs, jackdaws, tortoises, rabbits, monkeys, chickens, quail, cats, pigeons and magpies. Ovid even wrote movingly on the death of a pet parrot: 'He was all his life long a faithful friend who never wavered in his loyalty.' *ELEGIES,* 6

The philosopher Porphyry brought a quail back from Carthage with him. It would answer back when he 'discoursed' with it, and would stay silent when he wanted quiet.

Snakes were working 'pets', and many Roman households had a domestic snake to keep down vermin. In fact the emperor Tiberius not only kept a snake as a pet, he used to feed it from his own hand.

If my friend Flaccus delights in a long-eared owl ...
If Publius is passionately fond of his little puppy
And Cronius loves the ape that so looks like himself,
If a mischievous lizard gratifies Marius;
If a talkative magpie pleases Lausus;
If Glaucilla twines an icy snake round her neck;
If Tetania has built a tomb for a nightingale ...
[We see that] strange things bring pleasure.

MARTIAL, *EPIGRAMS,* 7.87

TOTALLY ASININE

Elithio Phoitete remarked that he was the unluckiest of men, for no sooner had he trained his donkey to live without food than the beast suddenly died.

TRADITIONAL JOKE FROM ANCIENT GREECE

THE LEGEND OF BUCEPHALUS

Bucephalus was a magnificent horse, midnight-black and large-bodied, with 'a skull as wide as a bull's' (which is what 'bucephalus' means). He was also unmanageable, becoming frightened and savage as soon as anyone tried to mount him. He was offered to King Philip of Macedon, but the king's trainers could do nothing with him. This caused Philip's young son to remark disparagingly: 'If those men just paid a bit of attention and showed some boldness then such a fine horse would not be lost.' He went on to claim: 'I could manage that horse.'

Macedonian kings had a somewhat relaxed attitude to health and safety as applied to princes, so the 12-year-old was allowed to try taming the stallion, though on the understanding that if he failed – and survived – he would have to pay for the horse himself. The boy had observed that the horse was frightened of his own shadow. When he turned it to face the sun and spoke soothingly to it, he was able to mount it.

The boy grew up to be Alexander the Great, and Bucephalus carried Alexander on the campaigns that conquered the Persian empire, getting through all his many battles without a scratch.

Bucephalus died on the banks of the Hyspades river (in modern-day Pakistan) when Alexander fought his last battle in 326 BC. By some reports Bucephalus died in the battle, though the historian Arrian says that old age and exertion did the deed – if, as legend claimed, Bucephalus and Alexander were born in the same year, then Bucephalus had indeed come to the end of his natural life.

A town called Bucephala (believed to be modern Jhelum) was founded near the site of the old warhorse's last battle.

Alexander and Bucephalus.

ANCIENT ANIMALS AND THEIR HUMANS

JULIUS CAESAR'S HORSE

He rode a remarkable horse, too, with feet that were almost human; for its hoofs were cloven in such a way as to look like toes. This horse was foaled on his own place, and since the soothsayers had declared that it foretold the rule of the world for its master, he reared it with the greatest care, and was the first to mount it, for it would endure no other rider. Afterwards, too, he dedicated a statue of it before the temple of Venus Genetrix. SUETONIUS, *LIFE OF CAESAR*, 61

SEIUS' HORSE

In the last days of the Roman Republic one Gnaeus Seius had a horse so magnificent that it was alleged to come from the accursed stock of the legendary Diomedes. And there may have been some truth in this, since all of its owners met grisly ends. Seius was condemned to a 'most cruel death' by Mark Antony, while Cornelius Dollabella, who purchased the horse on his way to Syria, died soon after. Gaius Cassius, whose men had killed Dollabella, took the horse just before he died at Philippi, and finally Mark Antony himself sought out the (in)famous horse, and soon after died ignominiously in Egypt.

For the next few hundred years anyone suffering unusual misfortune was said to 'have the horse of Seius'.

CALIGULA'S HORSE

No matter how many times the story is repeated, it is still not true that Caligula made his horse a consul of Rome. The fable originates in a throwaway remark in Suetonius' *Life of Caligula* (5), in which the imperial biographer reports how the emperor doted on the horse:

On the day before the races he used to send his soldiers to enforce silence in the neighbourhood, so that his favourite horse, Incitatus ['Swift'], might be able to rest peacefully. Besides a stall of marble, a manger of ivory, purple blankets and a collar of precious stones, he even gave this horse a house, with a retinue of slaves and fine furniture, all the more elegantly to entertain the guests invited in the horse's name.

Suetonius – who is not usually shy of reporting scandal as solid fact – here adds cautiously: 'It is also said that he intended to make him consul.'

SERTORIUS' FAWN

According to Plutarch, the rebel Sertorius had a fawn that was particularly rare, as its coat was milk-white. He was presented with the fawn as a gift and trained it to come when he called and follow him wherever he went, even through the tumult of an army camp.

Sertorius claimed that the fawn had been sent to him by the goddess Diana, and he pretended to his superstitious Lusitanian warriors that it was a supernatural beast that told him secrets of where the enemy were and the best time to attack. Whenever he had news of a victory, he would hide the messengers from his men until he had announced that the fawn had foretold good news.

A Julio-Claudian prince on horseback.

FEELING A BIT HORSE

A Scythian chieftain was killed by an enemy in single combat, but when the victor dismounted and came to strip his opponent of his armour he was killed by the kicks and bites of the dead chieftain's horse.

PLINY THE ELDER, *NATURAL HISTORY*, 8.75

ANCIENT BIRDS AND THEIR HUMANS

HONORIUS' HEN

Honorius was Roman emperor at the start of the fifth century AD. He was something of a birdbrain, so it is unsurprising that his favourite pets were chickens. He was particularly fond of a bird called Roma. At this time Rome, the city that the bird was named after, was no longer the imperial capital – instead, faced by the barbarian hordes, the imperial court had retreated to the safety of Ravenna. When the inevitable happened, and barbarian armies sacked Rome in AD 410, a messenger brought the news to the emperor with the dramatic announcement: 'Rome has perished!'

'But I was feeding her an hour ago!' protested the horrified emperor, who on receiving an explanation, was allegedly relieved that the news was not as bad as he had thought.

LESBIA'S SPARROW

> Sparrow, my girl's favourite,
>   she is accustomed to play with you,
> and hold you in her lap,
>   she gives your greedy beak her index finger
>   and provokes sharp bites.
> ...
> If only I could play with you as you do that bird
>   and ease sad care from your mind.
>
> CATULLUS, *CARMINA*, 2

It is suggested that rather than a standard sparrow (and somewhat transparent metaphor), Lesbia's pet was actually a piping bullfinch. Not that Romans were averse to sparrows either – there is a reference to *Passer in Sarcophago* in Roman cookery, which seems to be a sparrow baked in a puff pastry 'coffin'.

COMMODUS AND OSTRICHES

The emperor Commodus used to show off by shooting ostriches with specially made crescent-shaped arrows that would decapitate the birds so neatly that for a while they would continue running as though nothing had happened.

HERODIAN, *HISTORY OF THE EMPIRE*, 1.15.5

Here is another thing that he [Commodus] did to us senators that gave us every reason to look for our death. Having killed an ostrich and cut off his head, he came up to where we were sitting, holding the head in his left hand and in his right hand raising aloft his bloody sword and though he spoke not a word, yet he wagged his head with a grin, indicating that he would treat us in the same way.

And many would indeed have perished by the sword on the spot, for laughing at him (for it was laughter rather than indignation that overcame us), if I had not chewed some laurel leaves that I got from my garland, and persuaded the others who were sitting near me to do the same, so that in the steady movement of our jaws we might conceal the fact that we were laughing.

EPITOME OF CASSIUS DIO, 72.21

GODS AND THEIR BIRDS

The dove is sacred to Aphrodite

The owl and goose to Athena*

The eagle to Jupiter

The raven to Apollo

*It is from the connection between Athena and the goose that we get the Mother Goose stories

*Geese on the side of a
Roman altar.*

THE DOLPHIN THAT LIKED HUMANS TOO MUCH

A boy in the small town of Hippo Diarrhytus on the African coast went swimming one day ...

He was met by a dolphin, who sometimes swam in front of him, and sometimes behind him, then played round him, and at last took him upon his back ... This he did the next day, the day after, and for several days together, till the people ... dared to get closer, playing with him and calling him to them, while the dolphin, in return, allowed himself to be touched and stroked. After a while familiarity made them brave. The boy, in particular, who first met the dolphin swam side by side with him, and leaping upon his back, was carried backwards and forwards in that manner, and thought the dolphin knew him and was fond of him, while he too had grown fond of the dolphin. PLINY THE YOUNGER, *LETTERS*, 107

Taras riding a dolphin.

The story has a tragic end, for so many important visitors came to see this remarkable dolphin that the town nearly bankrupted itself in paying for and entertaining them. In the end, deciding that the town was enjoying more fame than it could take, the city fathers arranged for the unsuspecting dolphin to be killed.

THE FLYING FRANKINCENSE SNAKES

The trees which produce frankincense are guarded by winged serpents. These are small and of various colours, but they watch in great numbers about each tree ... and they cannot be driven away from the trees by anything except [a certain kind of] smoke.

HERODOTUS, *THE HISTORIES*, 3.107

OPHIDIAN VENGEANCE

Snakes generally go in couples; nor can a snake live without its mate. If one is killed, it is incredible how the other will at all costs seek revenge, overcoming all difficulties.

PLINY THE ELDER, *NATURAL HISTORY*, 8.45

FAITHLESS BIRDS

[Dreams about] partridges signify both men and women, but generally godless, unholy women who are never kind to the men who support them. For partridges are hard to tame, speckled, and they alone of the birds have no respect for the gods.

ARTEMIDORUS DALDIANUS, *THE INTERPRETATION OF DREAMS*, 4.46

THE LIFE OF THE CAMEL

According to Aristotle, 'camels live for about 30 years; in some exceptional cases they live much longer, and there are cases known where they have lived to be 100.' In fact, an average camel lives for two score years, and if particularly healthy, two score and ten. The world record is apparently 80, though this is uncertain. However, Aristotle is even more wildly out – and more sceptical – with elephants: 'They say the elephant lives for about 200 years – but according to other accounts for 300.' Elephants are indeed relatively long-lived, but don't even make it through one century – it's a really lucky elephant that sees 90.

THE HISTORY OF ANIMALS, 8.9

Dromedary.

ELEPHANT ROUND-UP

THE ELEPHANT OF KING PORUS

The same battle which was Bucephalus' last (see p. 113), saw Alexander's army facing some 200 elephants under the command of King Porus, who personally led his army into battle on the back of an elephant. When, after a bitter fight, Porus' army was defeated, the severely wounded king slipped from his elephant to the ground. The mahout, thinking the king was dismounting, ordered the elephant to kneel. The elephant did, and the example of the royal steed was followed by the surviving members of the elephant cavalry. In this way the elephants inadvertently offered their surrender to the approaching Macedonians. But when the royal elephant saw Alexander's men advancing on his master, he lifted the body onto his back and prepared to defend it.

Porus survived the battle, was complimented by Alexander on his bravery, and restored to his kingdom. As for the elephant, history records two different outcomes. If Philostratus is to be credited, Alexander also ordered the elephant to be honoured for its gallantry; Plutarch, however, says that King Porus' elephant died defending him.

SURUS, HANNIBAL'S BRAVEST ELEPHANT

Hannibal took 37 elephants through the Alps, but where he got them is something of a mystery. Most scholars have speculated that Hannibal must have used a now-extinct North African species, since the surviving African elephant is a large and ferocious beast that is almost impossible to tame. Indian elephants are much more tractable, but live too far away. And besides, the one elephant that did come from the east was known by his distinctive origin as Surus ('the Syrian').

Surus distinguished himself with his bravery in the Battle of the River Trebbia, and thereafter became Hannibal's personal mount, carrying him through the swamps of Etruria while Hannibal himself was desperately sick and a ferocious winter had carried off the other elephants in the army. Surus was so well known to the Romans who opposed him that he gets a mention in Cato the Elder's *Origins*, one of the first histories ever written by a Roman, though Cato famously did not mention any Romans by name in his work. The elder Pliny tells us that Surus had only one tusk, which another Roman writer, Ennius, made into a joke: 'Though Surus carried only one stake, nevertheless they were able to defend themselves [with it].' The word 'surum' could also mean a sharp wooden stake that each Roman legionary carried to add to the defences of the ramparts when the army made camp.

A MOUNTAIN PASSAGE

Hannibal's crossing of the Alps is not the only mountain adventure involving elephants. In 169 BC a Roman general called Marcus Philippus crossed the mountains into Macedonia with about two dozen elephants in a hare-brained military adventure.

It was hard enough to get the elephants up the mountains, but getting them to go down the precipitous slopes looked even more of a challenge. In the end, the engineers with the Roman army came up with a solution. They built a bridge to nowhere – a walkway leading out over the mountain slope that finished several yards above the ground, but was at least reasonably level going while it lasted. The elephants were willing to walk along the flat bit, whereupon the engineers pulled out the props so that the ramps fell slowly to earth at the same inclination as the slope. The elephants then had no choice but to slide into Macedonia on their haunches, along with the rest of the Roman army.

POMPEY AND THE ELEPHANTS

Pompey the Great did not have a lot of luck with elephants and since he used them only for self-aggrandizement, he did not deserve to either. In 81 BC, as a young man, Pompey fought a successful campaign in North Africa during which he captured a number of elephants. It seemed a good idea for the young general to impress the people of Rome by taking the starring part in the procession in a chariot pulled not by horses, but by these elephants. The parade had already started when Pompey's chariot reached the city gate – which was too small for the elephants. After much toing and froing, Pompey had to make do with the traditional horses, and parade through the city to the mocking comments of his soldiers (who were dissatisfied with the share of the booty he had given them).

In 46 BC Caesar showed how it should be done. His triumphal chariot was the standard four horsepower version, but it was flanked by 40 elephants carrying torches with their trunks.

Worse was to follow for Pompey in 55 BC, when Pompey decided to stage spectacular games to celebrate the opening of his new theatre. Eighteen elephants were sent into the arena to fight to the death against men with javelins. These elephants were mostly tame, and when the humans attacked them their distress and confusion was so evident and pathetic that the crowd were immediately on their side. When the last had died, the crowd rose and solidly booed and shouted abuse at Pompey – which, after his trouble and expense, was hardly the effect he had been looking for.

NATURAL DISASTER

There was a town in Spain that was utterly destroyed
when it was undermined by rabbits.

PLINY THE ELDER, *NATURAL HISTORY*, 8.54

BLESS THE BEASTS

Elithio Phoitete is talking with two friends. One says:
'We are wrong to slaughter sheep, for they provide us with wool
for our clothes and blankets.' The other adds: 'We should not
kill the cow, which provides us with milk and cheese.'
Elithio agrees: 'And we should not kill the pig either, because
it provides us with such choice cuts of meat.'

TRADITIONAL JOKE FROM ANCIENT GREECE

ROMAN COOKERY

Thrushes (Turdes) Those from Spain were particularly flavoursome

Snails The larger, the better, and preferably fattened on milk

Dormice Several recipes exist

Sows' udders Try the tasty 'Trojan Horse', where the udder is stuffed with different meats

THE BLESSED STORK

The people of ancient Thessaly revered storks, which, they believed,
prevented the country from being plagued by snakes, and anyone
who killed a stork was banished forthwith.

PLUTARCH, *MORALIA*, 4.74

THE CHAMELEON

Of this creature, Pliny accurately reports: 'But the nature of its colour is more wonderful; for every now and then it changes it, as well in the eyes as the tail and the whole body. Whatever colour it touches it takes on the same colour, unless the colour is red or white.' However, he ruins an otherwise accurate description by saying: 'It is the only animal that needs neither food or drink, but lives completely on air.' PLINY THE ELDER, *NATURAL HISTORY*, 8.61

APPLES TO GO

Hedgehogs also prepare their provisions for winter. They roll themselves upon apples that lie on the ground, and which thus become fixed on their spines. Then they take an extra apple in their mouth and carry them to their homes in hollow trees.

PLINY THE ELDER, *NATURAL HISTORY*, 8.65

THE BEAR

The bear, a most fierce and ugly beast, brings forth her young shapeless and without limbs, but with her tongue, as with a tool, she shapes these limbs, so that she seems not only to bring forth but actually to sculpt her young. [Hence the modern expression, 'to lick into shape'.]

PLUTARCH, *ON NATURAL AFFECTION TOWARDS ONE'S OFFSPRING*, 2

The Roman emperor Valentinian I kept two she-bears named Goldflake and Innocence in a cage near his bedroom. He used the bears to dispose of troublesome petitioners and other reprobates.

AMMIANUS MARCELLINUS, *HISTORY*, 29.3.9

CATS

Cats were so revered in Egypt that a mob there lynched a Roman ambassador who accidentally killed one.

DIODORUS SICULUS, *HISTORICAL LIBRARY,* 1.83

In Rome, the statue of the goddess Libertas (liberty) had a cat at its feet, since the Romans believed that of all animals, the cat was the most free.

ANIMALS FROM AFAR

Which were reported to exist, but did not:

THE MANTICORE
If we are to believe Ctesias, the Indian wild animal known as the manticore has a triple row of teeth in both the upper and the lower jaw. This creature is as big and as hairy as a lion. Its paws too are leonine, but the head and ears are as a man's. The eyes are blue, and its colour vermilion; its tail is like a scorpion's, with a sting. Except that it also has spines that it is able to shoot off like arrows. Its voice sounds like something between a panpipe and a trumpet. It can run as fleetly as deer, and it is savage and a man-eater.
ARISTOTLE, *THE HISTORY OF ANIMALS*, 2.1

THE MAN-EATING GIANT GOLD-MINING ANTS OF INDIA
There are ants smaller than dogs but larger than foxes. These ants live underground ... the sand that they dig out has gold in it. The Indians go into the desert to get this sand. Each of the prospectors takes three camels. ... They deliberately set out at the hottest time of the day, when the heat has driven the ants underground. ... The Indians fill their bags with sand and then run for home as fast as they can. HERODOTUS, *THE HISTORIES*, 3.102 FF

THE SCYTHIAN BATTLING CRANE
These birds migrate from the steppes of Scythia to the marshlands south of Egypt at the source of the Nile. And it is here, incidentally, that they are said to fight with the pygmies. This is no fable – the little men really do exist. They live in underground caves and have horses that are likewise proportionately small. ARISTOTLE, *THE HISTORY OF ANIMALS*, 9.12

THE STRIX
A sort of bird that has a large fierce head, sharp beak, and claws like fish-hooks. They are nocturnal and find their prey when babies sleep uncared for by their nurses. They use the claws to tear out the baby's entrails and drink mother's milk mixed with blood from the stomach. Their cry by night fills men with horror. OVID, *THE FESTIVALS*, 6

NAMES FOR DOGS

Xenophon, in *On Hunting* (7.5), gives the following names for dogs:
Psyche, Thymus, Porpax, Styrax, Lonché, Lochus, Phrura, Phylax,
Taxis, Xiphon, Phonax, Phlegon, Alcé, Teuchon, Hyleus, Medas,
Porthon, Sperchon, Orgé, Bremon, Hybris, Thallon, Rhomé,
Antheus, Hebe, Getheus, Chara, Leusson, Augo, Polyeus, Bia,
Stichon, Spudé, Bryas, Oenas, Sterrus, Craugé, Caenon, Tyrbas,
Sthenon, Aether, Actis, Aechmé, Noës, Gnomé, Stibon, Hormé.

Ovid, in *Metamorphoses* (3.206–225) adds the following:
Melampus, Ichnobates, Pamphagus, Dorceus, Oribasos,
Nebrophonos, Theron Laelaps Pterelas, Agre, Hylaeus, Nape
Poemenis, Harpyia Ladon, Dromas, Canache, Sticte, Tigris, Alce,
Leucon, Astobolos, Lacon, Aëllo, Thoos, Lycisce, Cyprius,
Harpalos, Melaneus, Lachne, Labros Argiodus, Hylactor.

Classicists looking to name their mutt are particularly
commended to Polyeus ('Rover') and Sticte ('Spot').

Some names are evocative – for example, Aëllo ('Whirlwind') –
while others are descriptive (Asbolos, meaning 'Sooty'). Other
dogs are named after their characteristics such as Celer ('Swift')
and Ferox ('Savage') in Columella's *On Agriculture*.

Pliny reports that once in the reign of Tiberius a dog refused to
leave the body of his executed master 'but kept up a most piteous
howling beside it. Many Romans gathered to see this, and when
one of them threw the dog a piece of meat, he carried it to the
mouth of the corpse. When the dead body was thrown into the
Tiber, the dog swam after it, trying to keep it afloat.'
PLINY THE ELDER, *NATURAL HISTORY*, 8.70

Cave canem, *mosaic from Pompeii.*

DOGS

*Make much of your sharp-fanged
dog. Feed him generously,
so that the man who sleeps by day
does not make off with your
possessions by night.*

HESIOD, WRITING IN ABOUT 800 BC,
WORKS AND DAYS, 604–605

*Alcestis died for her husband;
but your modern woman would
let her husband go to Hades if it
could save her lapdog!*

JUVENAL, *SATIRES*, 6

*The Colophonians possessed squadrons of war-dogs that
were put in the front of the battleline, and were never known
to retreat. These they called their trustiest auxiliaries, and
ones that never needed pay.*

PLINY THE ELDER, *NATURAL HISTORY*, 8.69

A FAREWELL TO A FAITHFUL FRIEND

Parthenope his dog, with whom in life
It was his wont to play, Anaxeos here
Hath buried; for the pleasure that she gave
Bestowing this return. Affection, then,
Even in a dog, possesseth its reward,
Such as she hath who, ever in her life
Kind to her master, now receives this tomb.
See, then, thou make some friend, who in thy life
Will love thee well, and care for thee when dead.

INSCRIPTION BY ANAXEOS OF LESBOS ON THE TOMB OF HIS DOG

VIII

Odd Jobs

Society in antiquity was different in many ways from the modern world, and therefore different skills were in demand. We might wonder at the profession of armpit plucker, but the Romans would have been just as bemused by life coaches and aromatherapists. While changing times have made some professions redundant, others, such as the *delator* – who made a living by denouncing suspicious types to the authorities – seem on the verge of making a comeback. This chapter explores some of the more curious career options in the ancient world.

Roman fuller (see p. 141).

THE ARMY

SAPPER

For these soldiers, 'the underground war' meant not secret codes and resistance fighters but literally going underground with a shovel. The purpose was to dig out the foundations of a besieged city's walls and replace them with oil-soaked timber props. Then just before an attack, the sappers would light the props. When these burned through, they collapsed the walls under their startled defenders. The defenders naturally took a dim view of this, and went to great lengths to locate sappers' tunnels. They might then send counter-sappers down, or a welcoming party that included infuriated wasps and a wild bear or two. Or they might simply pump oily smoke into the tunnel and suffocate their attackers.

WELL-TEMPERED

Swords were made more flexible by prolonged heating of the iron to high temperatures with charcoal. The carbon from the charcoal was absorbed by the hot iron which became steel.

THE DOCS OF WAR

A physician is more valuable than several other men combined; he's the one who can cut out arrows and spread herbs which heal.

HOMER, *THE ILIAD*, BK 11

Battle Elephant Driver

Those who propelled an elephant into battle needed to know the character of their temperamental charge. While an excited elephant was sudden death if it fell on ranks of close-packed infantry, an over-excited elephant did not much care which side that infantry belonged to. To stop a berserk elephant from wreaking havoc on his comrades, every elephant driver carried a sharp chisel and a hammer. If the worst came to the worst he would attempt to whack the chisel into the elephant's brain as it rampaged through his own army.

Elephants attached to a chariot and bearing a tower.

Anti-elephant Infantrymen and Pig Igniters

Given the potential destruction a well-aimed elephant could cause, and the demoralizing effect they had on those who faced them, it is no surprise that considerable ingenuity went into getting enemy elephants off the battlefield before they did any harm. Tactics ranged from the basic shower of fire arrows to the more desperate measure of setting fire to a tar-coated pig and sending the squealing fireball bounding towards the approaching pachyderms. Few jobs could have required more courage than that of the anti-elephant corps of Perseus of Macedon, whose warriors wore armour with sharp spikes bristling from the front and back in the hope that elephants would find attacking these men the equivalent of a human running barefoot over a lawnful of hedgehogs.

BALLISTA OPERATOR

Firing a catapult was a complex business, but the operator's skills did not stop there. Apart from some specialist equipment, most siege artillery was built on the spot, so the ballista operator needed good engineering skills. When the time for an assault came, the operator would have a set of rocks lined up for throwing, each carefully graded for weight and range; sometimes they were also painted so that they did not show up against the sky and give the human targets time to duck. It was probably the dream of most operators to fire off a shot as serendipitous as that when a commander ordered the head of a captured enemy general to be fired over the city walls. It landed smack in the middle of a council of the surviving generals, who were debating whether to continue with their resistance.

Operating the machine was not without peril as this quote from the historian Ammianus Marcellinus shows:

In the course of these struggles [against the Persians] one of the operators loaded a stone insecurely onto the sling of a scorpion. One of our builders (whose name I can't remember) happened to be standing behind when the stone was hurled backward. The poor man was thrown onto his back and killed. His chest was crushed and his limbs were torn apart so comprehensively that not even bits of his whole body could be identified. AMMIANUS MARCELLINUS, *HISTORY*, 24.4.28

Two main types of ballista were the 'scorpion' – essentially a gigantic crossbow – and the later onager, a spring-loaded catapult that bucked so violently as it released its load that it resembled the mule (onager) from which its name was derived.

Roman artillery piece.

SIEGE TOWER FIREMAN

Siege warfare was common in the ancient world, and was a sophisticated and specialist business. One way of getting over a high city wall was to build a siege tower – essentially a mini-skyscraper on wheels. These towers – some up to six storeys tall – were pushed towards the wall by soldiers who then climbed to the top and over the wall. The enemy naturally did their best to destroy the tower, often using flaming arrows and boiling oil. Those charged with keeping the tower unburned would cover it with wet cow skins, and stand within it during the advance, wielding fire extinguishers with hoses made of pickled cow intestines.

RANKS IN THE ROMAN LEGION, IN ASCENDING ORDER

Munifex The very bottom of the heap

Immunis As the name says, excused from some of the nastier jobs

Principalis In line for promotion to centurion

Optio Centurion's understudy

Centurions have a complicated hierarchy of their own:

Primus Pilus Top dog centurion in this complicated hierarchy

Military Tribune Often an auxiliary officer brought into the legion

Praefectus Castrorum The man who actually runs the legion on a day-to-day basis

Tribunus Laticlavus Understudy to the Legate

Legate The man in charge of the legion

(Officially all ranks below centurion were simply legionaries, but some legionaries were more equal than others.)

Opposite *Frieze of dancing girls.*

ENTERTAINMENT

Symposium Performer

A symposium was an occasion for Greek men to get together in a private house and discuss life, the universe and everything. Or to get drunk while watching a good floor show. These floor shows were provided by professional troupes, and the writer Xenophon described one in which a girl danced on a potter's wheel, and two young actors performed the romance of Dionysus and Ariadne so ardently that the symposium broke up soon afterwards as the men 'hurried home to the pleasures of the marriage bed'. On less restrained occasions, the proceedings might well have degenerated (or improved, depending on one's viewpoint) into an impromptu orgy, in which the performers would have been expected to participate.

BUSTUARIA

Rome had swarms of prostitutes catering for every taste and class. Those ladies of the night who could afford nowhere else to entertain customers 'borrowed' accommodation in tombs for this purpose. Hence the nickname bustuaria, *which means 'grave-watcher'.*

CHARIOTEER

'Live fast die young' could have been the motto of those who drove in tiny chariots behind a team of semi-demented horses at high speed. Chariot racing was a long-established sport – it was one of the prestige events at the ancient Olympics – but it reached it peak of popularity in the Circus Maximus in Rome. During the first years of the Roman empire, hundreds of thousands turned out to watch charioteers in action. The rewards were great ('You'll get for a year what a chariot driver earns in a single race,' Juvenal remarks to a schoolteacher in one of his poems), but so were the risks as this verse by the poet Martial shows:

> Scorpus, darling of the roaring Circus,
>   wildly applauded, but short lived.
> Snatched away by spiteful fate
>   when only 26 years old.
> Fate counted by victories, not by years,
>   and that made you an old man. What injustice!
> You have been robbed of your youth, Scorpus,
>   and all too soon have harnessed the dark horses of death.
> Time and again you hurried to cross the finish line,
>   why does it now have to mark the limit of your life?

MARTIAL, *EPIGRAMS*, 10.53

When Felix, an immensely popular charioteer, was being cremated, Pliny reports that a distraught fan died by throwing himself into the funeral pyre.

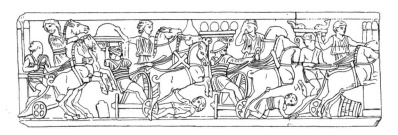

TYPES OF ROMAN GLADIATOR

Cimachaeri Fighters who use two short swords

Equites Gladiators on horseback

Essedari Gladiators in chariots

Hoplomachi Greek-style hoplites, who often fight Thracians

Laquerii Cowboys of the arena, with a lasso

Mirmillones Another type who fight *Hoplomachi* or Thracians

Retiarii The classic, fighting with trident, dagger and net

Secutores Fighters with a shield, helmet and sword. Their standard opponents are the *Retiarii*

Samnites Armed, as were Rome's Italian foes, with a rectangular shield, helmet and short sword

Thracians Fight with a round shield and curved dagger

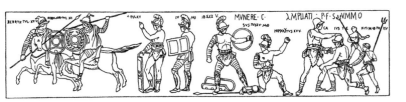

Above *Gladiators in action.* **Opposite** *Chariot races. Of these two forms of mass entertainment in Rome, chariot racing was probably the more popular.*

LANISTA

While the glamour of the arena made gladiators into the popular icons of their day, many gladiators who came second in a bout found that their pension plan was a waste of effort. The risks involved in combat with a well-armed, highly trained man whose life depended on killing the person he was fighting persuaded many that there was a better career to be had in training and preparing such gladiators for the arena. Sadly, unlike the idolized gladiator, the professional *lanista* was an object of popular scorn and contempt, while wealthy amateurs who kept a troupe of gladiators were praised if their fighters performed well.

THEATRE SHADE OPERATOR

Greek and Roman plays were performed in daylight, and given the scorching temperatures of a Mediterranean summer, a shade protecting the audience from the sun was deeply appreciated. The larger the theatre, the more skill was needed to manipulate the shade, and those at the peak of the profession were sailors from the Roman fleet at Misenum who had the job of unfurling the huge sunshade that protected the audiences at the Colosseum. (The shade did not cover the arena itself, but those participating in events had more than sunburn to worry about.)

Greek acrobats. Acrobatic performances were among the acts staged between chariot races at the Circus Maximus, hence the word 'circus'.

DEUS EX MACHINA

Literally the 'god from the machine'. This was the actor who was strapped to a winch in the upper parts of the theatre and lowered onto the stage in a Greek play to divinely sort out the tangled mess the plot had got into. This convenient way of resolving a play rapidly became such a hackneyed contrivance that the 'deus' was as likely to be met by a chorus of boos as by a reverent silence.

COMMERCE

MERCHANT ADVENTURER

In Queen Victoria's empire it was said that 'trade followed the flag'. In Caesar's empire, trade went well before the eagles, and on to places where the eagles never ventured. Roman merchants turned up at the courts of the Chinese emperor and had trading bases along the coast of India. The Romans never managed to conquer the Germans, but their merchants certainly managed to give them a taste for Mediterranean wines. Complete trading towns have been unearthed in Germany well beyond the limits of the empire, and it is an oddity of archaeology that most Roman swords have been found outside the empire. The Roman authorities did not like their citizens to go around armed, but unscrupulous merchants were quite happy to sell high-grade weapons to Rome's enemies.

PIRATE

The Mediterranean in ancient times was swarming with pirates. Some nations, such as the Illyrians of the Adriatic Sea, made piracy almost a national sport. One reason why many cities, including Athens and Rome, were built slightly inland was because of the risk of raiders descending unexpectedly from the sea. Pirates preyed not only on merchantmen, but also on the passengers they carried, who could be ransomed or sold as slaves. In fact, Julius Caesar was once captured by pirates, but was indignant at the size of the ransom they wanted for him, and insisted that it be substantially increased. Some of the most successful pirate ships had sails dyed in expensive purple, and oars tipped with silver.

Liquamen Manufacturer

The good part of this job is that you work on the coast of sunny Spain. The bad part is that you have to load chunks of fish (mackerel is best) into large shallow bowls full of spices and salt. Then wait for the fish chunks to ferment and dissolve in the sun over the next few weeks. Once nature has taken its course, strain the resultant mixture through a muslin cloth, package it, and send it off for sale and consumption in Greece and Italy.

> The little onyx pot held perfume
> Then Papylus sniffed at it
> And look, it's liquamen!
>
> MARTIAL, *EPIGRAMS*, 7.94

Container of liquamen in a mosaic from Pompeii.

Delator

Today these would be called informers. Anyone with solid evidence, or even a convincing fabrication, could report a political criminal to the authorities for a share in the about-to-be-deceased's estate. Indeed, one wealthy Roman, seeing his name on a list of those to be arrested commented sadly: 'Alas, I see my farm in the Alban Hills has told against me.' Unfortunately for the *delator*, the Roman authorities kept conscientious lists of those to whom they had made disbursements, and these were read avidly after a violent regime change. Sadly, even revolutionary governments could see the value of not fatally discouraging informers, and most *delators* merely had to give the money back.

In ancient Athens, the citizens were inordinately fond of their figs. Indeed these also enjoyed a high reputation abroad, and as Attica was neither large nor particularly productive, there were sometimes not enough figs to go round. It did not take long for an enterprising politician to seek popularity by banning the export of figs – leading, soon enough, to the emergence of fig-smugglers. The authorities rewarded those who gave information about such smugglers, and even today such informers – 'fig tellers' or 'sycophants' are a byword for sucking up to those in power.

SLAVE AUCTIONEER

In antiquity certain types of goods were commonly sold by auction – including human beings. It was the job of the auctioneer to talk up the good qualities of the product being sold while skipping lightly around the faults. Martial tells us of an auctioneer trying to sell a girl with a somewhat promiscuous reputation. To show her charms he gave her a passionate kiss – which resulted in the only bidder withdrawing his offer.

Elithio was asked by a friend that if he was going to the market, could he purchase two 15-year-old slaves. 'Certainly,' replied Elithio. 'And if I can't find two 15-year-olds at a good price, I'll buy you one 30-year-old.'

TRADITIONAL JOKE
FROM ANCIENT GREECE

Slave in chains. While some slaves, such as Cicero's Tiro, were almost friends of the family, many slaves were treated as poorly as farm animals.

THE *CURSUS HONORUM* – ROMAN MAGISTRACIES

Quaestor A junior magistrate, usually in charge of looking after finances for a more senior man. This was the lowest rank for entry into the Roman Senate

Tribune A rank only open to plebeians. Though relatively lowly on the cursus, a popular tribune was a formidable force

Aedile In charge of keeping the city functioning: keeping the streets clean, managing the infrastructure, and licensing various institutions, including brothels

Praetor A high executive post. Praetors might be in charge or armies and provinces or might have responsibilities in Rome. For example the *Praetor Urbanus* had legal responsibilities, and the *Praetor Peregrinus* who was responsible for foreigners in the city

Consul Originally there were two per year, but in the empire it became customary for consuls to resign during their turn in office and give someone else a go

Censor The most prestigious office in Rome, later monopolized by the emperor. Censors were in charge of registering citizens (hence the modern 'census') and managing state contracts

SENATORS ABROAD

Members of the Roman Senate required special permission from the emperor before they could leave Italy. Many, however, were commanded to leave on imperial business. Here are their posts in ascending order of importance:

Vingentivir Member of a panel of 20 senators with a brief in foreign affairs

Tribunus Laticlavus Understudy to a provincial governor or legion commander

Quaestor A junior senator, often in charge of financial affairs under the provincial governor

Praetor Often govern minor provinces, especially those without a legion

Legionary Legate Commander of a legion and therefore master of four per cent of the empire's armed forces

Imperial legate Governor of an imperial province, deputizing for the emperor

Proconsular governor Governor of a senatorial province as no one's deputy

Holder of *Maius Imperium* Outranking everyone in sight, including provincial governor (given the potential for trouble this rank had, most emperors kept it for themselves)

FULLER

A candidate for office in Rome was known by his gleaming white 'candida' toga. The man with the happy job of doing the whitening was the fuller. The ancients did not use soap to break down the grease in dirty clothing, but instead relied on a mix of acids and nitrates dissolved in water. A bonus was that this mixture was produced in abundance by unskilled labour – as urine. To collect their bounty, the fullers provided large containers on street corners. These containers were poured into narrow vats containing the garments. Then all that the fuller had to do was tramp the mixture in with his bare feet, before wringing the cloth dry and further bleaching it with sulphur smoke. Finally the cloth was scrubbed with fuller's earth – an ingredient of kitty litter even today – to remove the impurities, and sent off to the waiting candidate.

Roman fullers at work.

CASE STUDY

Then there was the grammarian whose daughter, after mingling in love, had a child who was masculine, feminine and neuter.

GREEK ANTHOLOGY, 9.489

POSSIBLE PROFESSIONS FOR WOMEN IN ANCIENT GREECE

Baker	Pharmacist	Laundrywoman
Fishmonger	Dancer	Market-stall owner
Priestess	Witch	Wet-nurse
Seamstress	*Hetaira*	Bath-house keeper
Musician	Prostitute	Camp-follower
Weaver	Innkeeper	

Greek ladies who spin and weave.

RELIGION

It has already been seen (in Chapter III) that religion in antiquity offered a wider range of options than those available in modern religion – for example, few priests today, of whatever persuasion, have the chance of predicting the divine will through careful examination of a sacrificial liver before settling down to eat that liver grilled with onions and parsley. Here are some other fields in which those from the twenty-first century need not apply:

Insignia of the Pontificate.

KANEPHOROS

This job was unpaid, but hardly required strenuous working hours. It was also one of the most prestigious jobs a woman in ancient Greece could perform, as the Kanephoros was the representative of her city during one of its great religious festivals. At the Great Panathenaia in Athens, for example, the Kanephoros led the citizens in their procession to the altar of Athena, the protective goddess of the city. She carried with her a basket (the job description is in the name, which means 'basket carrier') containing fruits, and on those occasions where an animal sacrifice was scheduled, the garlands with which the animal was to be adorned. Given the bragging rights that went with the job, there was intense competition for the honour, and only maidens of the highest reputation were accepted.

SOME TYPES OF ROMAN PRIEST

Pontifices In charge of state cults and the calendar. The *Pontifex Maximus* was close to being the chief priest of Rome

Flamines Each of the major gods had *Flamines* dedicated to their cult. The *Flamen Dialis* was a senior and ancient priesthood surrounded by taboos (see p. 55)

Libitinarii Served the grim goddess Libitina and dealt with death and funerals

Salii Another ancient priesthood charged with the rituals of war

Augurs Studied the movements of birds and beasts to understand divine intentions

Haruspices Studied the insides of birds and beasts after sacrifice to understand divine intentions

Fratres Arvales Blessed the fields and supervised boundaries

Corybantes Priests of the goddess Cybele, who had to be from Phrygia in Asia Minor, and be castrated

Vestal Virgins Served Vesta, goddess of the hearth. They could marry when they stood down, but sex on the job was punished by being buried alive

DOG-CRUCIFIER

The gruesome Roman habit of crucifying dogs goes back to 390 BC, when according to tradition the Gauls sneaked up Rome's Capitoline Hill in the hope of taking this last Roman stronghold, just as they had already taken and pillaged the rest of the city. Culpably, the guard dogs lay sleeping, and it was left to the sacred geese of the goddess Juno to raise the alarm. (Juno was henceforth known as Juno Moneta – 'Juno who gives warning' – and as the first Roman coins were struck under Juno's auspices, these coins were later known as 'money'.)

'A dog fastened to a cross, and a goose lying in a bed of state upon a rich cushion, are carried about, even to this day, in pompous solemnity,' Plutarch tells us in *The Fortune of the Romans*. Some callous individual had the job of nailing the unfortunate guard dog to a cross – a reminder of the Roman attitude to the cheapness of life, and that their indifference to suffering also extended to man's best friend.

PHALLUS MANUFACTURER

In a world where drought and famine were regular disasters, fertility was important. It was also vital to the farmer seeking to increase his flocks and the householder looking for children to protect him in old age. And what better representation of rampant life was there than the phallus? Consequently depictions of the phallus were everywhere in ancient Athens, and were regularly carried and waved enthusiastically in religious processions – in fact some of the more heroic versions were large enough to require two people to carry them. Fortunately the basic cylinder design allowed the manufacturer to use materials which were both light enough to be carried for long periods but still strong enough to avoid any droopiness which would have undone the entire point of the symbol.

ANCESTOR IMPERSONATOR

A treasured privilege of the Roman aristocracy was the *ius imaginem* – the right to keep wax masks of their ancestors. These masks were highly realistic for the simple reason that they were moulded on the face of the actual Roman as soon as he had died and become an ancestor. When yet another of the noble line had passed away, his family would give him a send-off with a funeral worthy of his status. Among those who followed in the funeral train would be the 'ancestors' of the deceased as represented by an actor wearing the appropriate mask. Thus the length of the train of mourning ancestors showed the antiquity of the family of the deceased. Julius Caesar's family claimed to go all the way back to the goddess Venus, though one might be excused for doubting the authenticity of the masks worn by the actors impersonating the earliest members of that clan.

THE JUDGE AND THE DOCTOR

Choose if you can
To be sentenced by Hegemon
The slayer of robbers
Rather than fall
Into the care
Of Gennadius the surgeon.

Hegemon executes killers
In his justified wrath
But Gennadius not only sends you to Hades
Gennadius also sends you a bill.

GREEK ANTHOLOGY, 9.280

IX

CRIMINAL RECORDS

Policemen were unknown in antiquity, where keeping order was the job of the authorities, and preventing crime was the job of ordinary citizens. A thief who was brought to justice could expect the authorities to take a very dim view of his activities, and in antiquity a 'suspended sentence' involved a noose or crucifix.

Roman slave receives an impromptu flogging.

THE BIGGEST GOLD HEIST – EVER

The Gauls once launched a raid on the Greek treasury at Delphi. Some of the gold is alleged to have ended up in the city of Tolosa (modern-day Toulouse), and was cursed as a result. Whether this is true or not, Tolosa was a sacred centre in Gaul and fabulously wealthy. So wealthy that when in 106 BC Quintus Servilius Caepio was sent to stop an invading German army, he took the time to conquer Tolosa and steal its treasure. This was sent to Rome under armed guard, but it mysteriously vanished along the way – all 210,000 pounds of gold and silver, worth about £35 billion in today's market. Many believed that Servilius Caepio had himself arranged the theft.

After capturing Tolosa, the proconsul Caepio removed 100,000 pounds of gold and 110,000 of silver from the temple of Apollo. After it had been sent off under guard to Marseilles, all of it is said to have been criminally made away with. There was a huge enquiry at Rome. OROSIUS, 5.15

NOT GUILTY

Nor do those who act unjustly think that they do wrong; indeed not, on the contrary some of them even persuade themselves that they are doing good.

PLUTARCH, *ON THE PASSIONS OF THE SOUL*, 3

CORNELIA THE POISONER

Ancient Rome was a far from healthy place, and it was fairly common for individuals inexplicably to fall sick and die. However, in 331 BC Rome seemed particularly accursed as many wealthy and well-connected individuals came down with an especially lethal malady. Eventually a maidservant revealed what was happening. She took a consul to the homes of a number of patrician ladies, some of whom were caught in the act of preparing suspicious-looking potions. In the end 20 of the women were brought to the Forum to face charges. Their leaders, the highly born Cornelia and Sergia (ancestors of the future Scipio Africanus and the rebel Catiline respectively), claimed that they were simply preparing healthy herbal drinks.

When asked whether they would like to demonstrate the health-giving qualities of their concoctions by drinking them, the women agreed. As they quickly died from the effects of the drink, it became apparent that they had agreed on a mass suicide to escape from justice.

Livy tells this story in his *History* (8.18) and says the women were evidently demented. More probably, given the intense rivalry among their families for office, these ladies had decided to form a club to thin the ranks of the competition.

THE MAIDEN AND THE HORSE

In Athens it was said that a man called Hippomenes decided that his daughter, a lass called Leimônê, had been unchaste. He locked her in a building with a horse until the animal was forced by starvation to eat the girl. So bizarre and cruel was her death that the building was referred to for generations thereafter as 'The maiden and the horse'.

TWO NOTICES ON THE WALLS OF POMPEII

From the Street of the Theatres: *A copper pot was taken from my shop. There is a reward of 65 bronze coins for anyone who brings it back. If they tell me where to seize the thief, they will get an extra 20.*

Near the door of the house of Pascius Hermes: *You, who keep crapping here, watch out for the curse! If you look down and see this, may Jupiter be your enemy!*

CIL 64 AND 7716

HEMLOCK

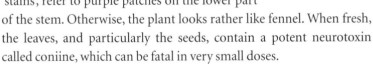

If you were sentenced to death in ancient Athens, one way to go was as Socrates did – with a swig of hemlock. (Not everyone enjoyed this privilege, strangulation was also used by the state.) Hemlock is obtained from the plant of the same name – though botanists call it *Conium maculatum*. The *maculae*, or *Deadly plant.* 'stains', refer to purple patches on the lower part of the stem. Otherwise, the plant looks rather like fennel. When fresh, the leaves, and particularly the seeds, contain a potent neurotoxin called coniine, which can be fatal in very small doses.

As a neurotoxin, hemlock works by slow paralysis that eventually stops the lungs, thus depriving the brain and heart of oxygen. Because hemlock is at its most potent in the spring and is much less effective once the plant has died or dried out, the official executioner would charge a considerable sum for those being killed out of season.

Greek doctors experimented with small doses of hemlock as a cure for arthritis, but the dose had to be exactly right. Most patients opted for living with the pain rather than risking death from the plant.

GOING TO LAW WITH AULUS GELLIUS

Aulus Hostilius Mancinus, a city magistrate of Rome, prosecuted a prostitute called Manilia because he had been struck with a stone thrown from her apartment one night. Manilia appealed to the tribunes saying that Mancinus had arrived in party clothes, and she would not let him in. Mancinus tried to break down the door and had to be driven off by stones. [The case was dismissed.] AULUS GELLIUS, *ATTIC NIGHTS*, 4.14

Euathlus the trainee lawyer agreed to pay his sponsor, the philosopher Protagoras, a certain sum of money on the day he won his first case. However, Euathlus attempted to avoid payment by never making a court appearance. At last Protagoras brought a lawsuit against him to recover the money. 'You have a problem,' explained the philosopher. 'If you lose this action, the court will award me the money; if you win it, you will have won your first case, and will owe me payment according to our agreement.' AULUS GELLIUS, *ATTIC NIGHTS*, 5.3

Chilo the Spartan was a judge with two others. Before the court was a friend on trial for his life. Chilo had to decide whether to sacrifice his friend – whom he knew to be guilty – or his lifelong dedication to justice. After long consideration, he squared the circle by voting for conviction, but persuading the other two judges to vote for an acquittal. AULUS GELLIUS, *ATTIC NIGHTS*, 1.3

A DEADLY BREACH OF CONTRACT

In 71 BC, Spartacus, the rebel gladiator, was cornered in the 'toe' of the Italian peninsula by the Roman legions. Though he had his back to the wall (or at least the sea), the ingenious Spartacus thought he could spot a way out. Just across the straits was Sicily, an island with a history of tumultuous slave uprisings. If only Spartacus could get his men across the strait, they would be massively reinforced by Sicilian slaves. Fortunately there was a small fleet of pirate ships operating in the area, who agreed to help.

Sadly, once they had taken Spartacus' money, the pirates sailed off without taking even one of the rebels on board. It is quite possible that they were paid to do this by the Roman commander, Publius Crassus, the richest man in Rome – thus receiving double payment without actually doing anything. Spartacus managed to fight his way out of the trap, but was cornered again near Brundisium and died in battle.

SHORT AND TO THE POINT

Ampliatus Pedania is a thief.

SCRIBBLED ON A WALL IN POMPEII, CIL 4993

Account books, bags of money and a casket of tickets.

DEALING WITH DEBT IN EARLY ROME

1 Once the magistrate has announced a man in default of a debt, the defaulter has 30 days to pay it off.

2 After the 30 days, if no one intervenes for the debtor, the creditor shall take him home and fasten him in chains.

3 He shall also secure the debtor with a weight of at least 15 pounds (7 kg), but more if he chooses.

4 The prisoner can arrange for his own food, but if not the creditor must give him at least a pound of meal a day.

5 On the third market day, the body of the debtor is divided among his creditors. If the creditors cut off more than their share of the debt, this is not a crime.

Table III of the Twelve Tables of Roman law.

THE TEN TOP THEFTS IN GREEK MYTHOLOGY

10 Theft of Ambrosia from the gods, by Pelops. Pelops was a mortal but a favourite of the gods, and he abused his position as cup-bearer to perform the theft.

9 The taking of the armour of Kronos, by Hades. Kronos was at war with his children, but they overcame him when Hades used his helmet of invisibility to steal Kronos' weapons. Hades' brother Zeus then became king of the gods.

8 The theft of the Golden Apples of the Sun, by Hercules. This task was given to Hercules in the hope that the monster who guarded the apples would destroy him.

7 The theft of the cattle of Apollo by Hermes. Done while the god was still an infant. Apollo got his cattle back, but exchanged them for the lyre which Hermes invented.

6 The theft of the horses of King Rhesus and the Palladium (a sacred statue) by Odysseus and Diomedes. These thefts were important to the Greek cause, as an oracular pronouncement said that Troy would not fall while these items were held by their original owners.

Jason and the Golden Fleece.

5 The theft of the Ceryrnthian Hind of Artemis – again by Hercules.
On the basis that a goddess might succeed in destroying Hercules
where monsters had failed, Hercules was ordered to steal the
hind of the goddess Artemis.

4 The theft of the Golden Fleece, by Jason and the Argonauts.
Jason had to steal the Golden Fleece from a sacred grove guarded
by a dragon to get his kingdom back.

3 The theft of Io (in the form of a heifer) from Argus, by Hermes.
Hermes had to steal a heifer (in reality a nymph with whom Zeus was
smitten) from hundred-eyed Argus. Hermes killed Argus, so Hera
transferred the watchman's eyes to the peacock's tail.

2 The abduction of Helen of Troy by Paris. The modern world might
call this elopement or kidnapping. In ancient Greece it was
woman-stealing.

1 The theft of fire from heaven by Prometheus. A gift that allowed
mankind to progress from savagery, but the gentle Titan Prometheus
suffered terribly when the gods discovered what he had done.

Abduction of Helen.

DEATH IN THE FAMILY

Nero was the last of the Julio-Claudian emperors of Rome. This was perhaps not a surprise, since Nero had done more than his fair share to make his family extinct. He was responsible for the deaths of his mother, two of his wives, his stepbrother and his own unborn child, and probably had a hand in the poisoning of his adoptive father, Claudius.

Claudius was the first to go, almost certainly poisoned by Nero's mother with Nero's knowledge. However, when the mother seemed to favour his stepbrother Britannicus, Nero had the young man poisoned at a banquet. (Nero claimed that Britannicus had died in an epileptic fit, but it rained during the funeral and this washed off the make-up that had been used to hide the characteristic lividity caused by the poison.)

Agrippina, his mother, was next, killed by Nero's soldiers. His wife, Octavia, whom Nero had married for political reasons, was divorced, then exiled, then put to death on a trumped-up charge of adultery. Nero's next wife, Poppea, he kicked to death after she reproached him for coming home late from the races – with her died their unborn child. When another noble Julio-Claudian, Antonia, quite reasonably refused to be his next wife, he had her executed as well for treason. Then, as his extravagance threatened to ruin Rome, Nero murdered his aunt (says Suetonius) so as to inherit her estate.

A young Nero and his mother Agrippina.

HAPPY FAMILIES IN PARTHIA

If the Romans thought their Julio-Claudians misbehaved, they had only to look east at the rival kingdom of Parthia to see how bad things could get:

- 62 BC Phraates III is assassinated by his sons Mithridates III and Orodes II
- 55 BC Orodes kills Mithridates
- 37 BC Phraates IV comes to power by killing his father Orodes (and 30 other sons of Orodes)
- 2 BC Phraates IV is murdered by his wife and his son Phraates V
- AD 2 Phraates V is killed in a rebellion when his marriage to his mother becomes public knowledge

ROYAL REVENGE

Astyges, king of the Medes, was very angry with one of his courtiers, called Harpagos, and dreamt up an especially gruesome punishment. Herodotus takes up the story:

When the son of Harpagos arrived, Astyges cut his throat and had the corpse disjointed, roasting some of the flesh and boiling other parts. Thus he had the body arranged and prepared for eating. And when the time came for the dinner, and Harpagos and the other guests had arrived, Astyges and the other guests had tables with mutton set before them, but Harpagos had the flesh of his own son, though the head, hands and feet were put aside and covered up in a basket. Then, when Harpagos had finished, Astyages asked him whether he had enjoyed the banquet.

When Harpagos replied that he had enjoyed it immensely, servants who had been instructed to do this beforehand brought the head, hands and feet still covered up, and asked Harpagos to take any leftovers that he desired. When Harpagos obeyed and uncovered the basket he saw the remains of his son. HERODOTUS, *HISTORIES*, 1.119

FOUR ANCIENT WHODUNNITS

WHAT KILLED GERMANICUS?

Caesar Germanicus was a charismatic general, a loving husband and father, and heir to the imperial throne. He and his family were the superstars of their day, idolized by millions. Then, while touring Rome's eastern possessions, he suddenly fell sick and died. On his deathbed Germanicus told friends that he had been poisoned by Piso and Plancina, respectively the governor of Syria and the governor's wife, with whom Germanicus had been feuding. Tacitus, a skilled forensic lawyer, later examined this case but believed there was not enough evidence to make a charge of poisoning stick, and said so in his *Annals* (2.75). Agrippina the Elder, wife of the deceased, was convinced her husband had been poisoned through the jealousy of the then emperor Tiberius. Modern theories include illness, especially malaria (Germanicus had just returned from Egypt), but any coroner's jury examining the case today would have to return an open verdict.

Coin of Germanicus.

LOVE IN ATHENS

In Athens, a man who had sex with any citizen woman to whom he was not married could be punished with death.

WHY WERE THE HERMS MUTILATED?

Herms were a deeply revered Athenian institution, consisting of square blocks or pillars of stone topped by a bearded face, and often with an imposing erection midway. Found in great numbers throughout Attica, the herms brought fortune to adventures, happy accidents and peril-free travel. Just as Athens was embarking on a huge military gamble by attacking Sicily, dozens of herms were disfigured in a night of vandalism. This act of violent blasphemy appalled the Athenians, and destroyed the career of one of the suspects, the flamboyant general Alcibiades. Though the desecration must have required considerable organization, the perpetrators were never found and their motives remain unknown. Historians have blamed this demoralizing attack on – among others – drunken vandals, Spartan agents and militant Athenian feminists.

WHO STARTED THE GREAT FIRE OF ROME?

In AD 64 a fire started in the area of the Circus Maximus in Rome. Fanned by favourable winds, the blaze tore through the densely packed houses at the foot of the Esquiline Hill, and spread out to envelop 11 of the 14 administrative districts of the city. It took almost a week to suppress the fire, after which the search for scapegoats began.

The immediate suspects were members of a Jewish millennial cult who believed that the end of the world was nigh, and were trying to hurry on events. The emperor Nero immediately ordered these cultists (called 'Christians') arrested and killed in various ingenious and gruesome ways. Nero was particularly keen to fix the blame on the Christians because an alternative theory was doing the rounds that Nero had himself authorized the fire as a drastic urban clearance scheme so that a more noble Rome might arise from the ashes.

Modern historians have tended to believe that the fire was an accident. However, Tacitus, who lived through the fire as a boy, says that eyewitnesses saw fire-starters at work. Certainly not all the members of Rome's large Jewish community were Christians of the turn-the-other-cheek persuasion. Some were radicals, incensed by Rome's occupation of their homeland and prepared to hit back at the 'Whore of Babylon' in any way they could.

Draco

In 620 BC the Athenians decided to establish a fixed code of laws. The job was given to an aristocrat called Draco, who, after codifying the various offences, ruled that the penalty for committing any of them should be death. When asked if this was not rather extreme, Draco replied that even the most minor of the offences merited death, while he could think of nothing worse for the others. Draco's laws were soon replaced, but the word 'Draconian' for an extreme official reaction has survived.

Crucifixion

The Greeks worked on the principle that the death sentence was needed to remove certain people from their society (and so they were often just as happy if the accused escaped from jail and exiled himself). The Romans, on the other hand, believed that criminals should die as gruesomely as possible, to deter others. Thus, crucifixion was practised throughout Rome's dominions. The accused was flogged and then fixed to a cross (hence the name, as *crux* means 'cross' in Latin). The victim then died slowly from shock and exposure. The horrendous agony of the process today survives in the word 'excruciating'.

Because the process could take days, guards had to be stationed to ensure that nobody attempted a rescue. It was not unknown for the guards to speed up the process, less through compassion than a desire to have the business over with and go home. Common methods included stabbing with a spear or breaking the victim's legs. The nails used in a crucifixion had considerable value afterwards as magical amulets.

WHAT HAPPENED TO ANTINOUS?

Antinous, the young, charming boy-lover of the emperor Hadrian, died while the pair were on holiday in Egypt. He drowned in the river Nile in very strange circumstances. First, the Nile at the point where Antinous entered it was rough and dangerous – not the sort of place one would go for a casual swim. Secondly, the emperor Hadrian described the incident with a Greek verb that can mean either 'he fell' or 'he was pushed'. Hadrian himself was somewhat unstable on the subject of Antinous, as evidenced by his hysterical grief afterward (he even tried, with reasonable success, to have Antinous deified).

Was Antinous killed during a lover's quarrel? Did he, knowing that Hadrian was attracted to boys, kill himself for fear of losing the emperor's love now that he was 18? Or did he willingly sacrifice himself to the Nile believing (as did many Egyptians) that such a death was sacred, and would confer benefits upon those – that is, Hadrian – for whom he had sacrificed himself?

Statue of Antinous.

PARRICIDE

In Rome, there was a very specific punishment for parricide, as the killing of a parent was regarded as the most horrible crime possible (followed closely by arson).

The condemned was sewn into a sack along with a snake, a cock, a dog and an ape, as these unfortunate animals were meant to embody the vices that had led to the crime in the first place. After the contents of the sack were given a good beating, the entire lot were thrown, still in the sack, into the Tiber to drown as an example to other would-be offenders.

A MUGGING IN ROME

It was one of the decadent pleasures of Nero to disguise himself as common riff-raff and wander the streets of Rome by night, attacking innocent citizens. He met his match in a senator called Julius Montanus, who defended himself fiercely until he discovered he was beating up his emperor. Nero had the man executed, and in future did his nocturnal attacks with a bodyguard of gladiators on stand-by in case he lost another fight. TACITUS, *ANNALS*, 13.21

A GHASTLY PUNISHMENT AT THE COLOSSEUM

Believe that Pasiphaë was mated with a Cretan bull:
we have seen it. The old story has been confirmed.

MARTIAL, *SPECTACLES*, 6

In Apuleius' The Golden Ass, the hero Lucius, magically transformed into a donkey, had to inflict a similar punishment on a poisoner in the arena. Apparently such events were rare enough for little oil lamps depicting the event to be sold as souvenirs of the occasion.

PUNISHMENTS IN ROME

Capital punishment:

Strangulation

Decapitation

Crucifixion

Drowning

Being thrown from the Tarpeian Rock

(After prisoners had been killed in the prison, their bodies were exposed on the nearby Gemonian Steps and eventually dragged by a hook to be thrown into the Tiber)

In the arena:

Ad bestias (thrown to wild beasts)

Noxi The condemned is killed by a fellow prisoner in the arena who is killed in turn by another, and so on

Dramatic performances Often the condemned is put in the role of a mythical character, usually to re-enact that character's last moments

Lesser punishments:

Fines

Public whipping

Sent to gladiator school

Property confiscated

Sent to the mines

Relegatio Sent to live in a specific place

Ad bestias. *Victims thrown to the beasts were generally tied to a post with details of their crime affixed above their heads.*

WANT SALT WITH THAT?

Anyone who fancies serving themselves can go and get a drink from the sea.

WARNING NOTICE IN THE BAR OF SALVIUS
IN POMPEII (CIL 3494)

PUNISHMENT FOR VESTAL NON-VIRGINS

For a Vestal Virgin of Rome to lose her virginity was an awful omen for the city – so much so that if something terrible happened to Rome, the chastity of the Virgins was immediately suspect. If a Virgin was found guilty of *incestum* (which to the Romans meant sacrilegious betrayal of an oath), the punishment was terrible. Still living, the unfortunate lady was taken through the city on her funeral bier to an underground chamber near the Colline Gate.

This single-use apartment had a lantern, some basic comforts such as a bed, and a small supply of food and drink. What it did not have, once the ex-virgin had entered it, was any exit or entrance. The hole was sealed and smoothed over so that it appeared that the victim had literally vanished off the face of the earth.

You call for a whip, Rufus,
claiming that your rabbit
has not been properly cooked.
You'd rather slice up your chef
than your rabbit.

MARTIAL, *EPIGRAMS*, 3.94

A slave is strung up and beaten while potters work.

What's for Dinner, Mum?

A wife hates the children of a concubine
No one can deny or forbid this statement
These days it's right and proper to kill a stepson
I warn you wards [of a stepmother]
(And especially if you have a rich estate)
Watch out for your lives!

Don't trust a single dish
Mother's apple pies
Are hot pastries
Black with poison.

Make sure someone else has first bite
Of whatever mother offers you
Give your trembling tutor
The first swig from every cup

... I wish these were idle words!
Yet who does not recall Pontia pronouncing
'Yes I did it, I confess, I did the deed
I poisoned my two children with aconite.
The crime was detected, and everyone knows of it.
With these hands I did it.'?

'What, you most savage viperess?
Two? You killed two at a single meal?'

'Oh yes, and I'd have killed seven
If there had been seven to kill.'
JUVENAL, *SATIRES*, 6

⇸ X ⇷

GOING IN
STYLE

We have all got to go some time –
here are some who went
very memorably.

*Funeral coin of
Pertinax.*

Petronius Arbiter

Petronius got the name of 'Arbiter' as he was the judge of elegance at the decadent court of Nero. (He is also believed to be the author of the scandalous *Satyricon* – a work of Roman literature emphatically not for minors.) Even when he fell out with the emperor and was sentenced to death in AD 66, Petronius did not lose his immaculate taste. Tacitus describes one of the most elegant suicides ever:

He was in no hurry to throw his life away. Instead, he cut open his veins and opened or bound up the wound as the mood took him. All the while, he was chatting with his friends. He was disdainful of topics that might give him a glorious reputation for courage, so the badinage was never serious. … Some of his slaves received generous presents for their services, others got a flogging. He ate well, and took care to sleep, for even though he was being forced to die, he wanted to make a good-looking corpse.

Even in his last will and testament he avoided the tendency of many others in their dying moments to flatter Nero, Tigellinus or others in high office. Instead he carefully detailed the emperor's debaucheries, the names of the men and women involved, and the novel tricks they had dreamed up [and if he was the author of the *Satyricon*, be assured that Petronius had the style and vocabulary to make the text fascinating reading]. He then sealed the document, and posted it off to Nero, afterwards breaking his signet ring, so that no messages could be sent in his name that might endanger others.
TACITUS, *ANNALS*, 16.19

OVERACHIEVER, PART 1

Metellus Macedonicus' funeral bier was carried by a serving Praetor of Rome. The other three pallbearers were ex-consuls, two of whom had celebrated a Roman triumph, and one of whom was a former censor. All four of these men, holders of the highest offices of the Roman Republic, were Metellus' sons.

ARRIA: LEADING BY EXAMPLE

Caecina Paetus got himself involved in a rebellion against the emperor Claudius in 42 BC. He was brought to Rome as a prisoner, but as an aristocrat and former consul of Rome, he was allowed the option of suicide to avoid condemnation and disgrace.

When Arria, his wife, was forbidden to accompany him on the boat taking him to Rome, she followed behind on a chartered fishing boat. Thus she was with her husband and comforted him during his last hours. When the time came, she set the tone by taking the sword left for the purpose and stabbing herself firmly in the chest. She then passed the sword to her husband, dying with the immortal last words: 'Paetus, it doesn't hurt.'

LEONIDAS, KING OF SPARTA

In 480 BC the Persian army of King Xerxes flooded into Greece, intent on conquest and revenge. Athens was frantically trying to evacuate its people, and armies were being mustered, but the cities of Greece needed time. It fell to King Leonidas of Sparta to buy that time – with his life. The Spartan king led 300 of Sparta's elite warriors to hold the pass at Thermopylae. He chose only men with sons, as he knew his soldiers were not coming back, and didn't want to wipe out any families.

Greek hoplite.

For a week the 300 held back the Persians, even though they were outnumbered roughly 10,000 to one. When their spears were shattered and their swords lost, the Spartans fought with their bare hands and teeth, and did not falter in their resistance until every man was dead. Xerxes knew well the value of that week to the Greeks, and his rage and frustration are shown by his treatment of the body of Leonidas. Usually the Persians treated defeated warriors according to their bravery, but the furious Xerxes ordered the corpse of Leonidas decapitated and the body crucified. This desecration was more than compensated by the honours heaped on his memory by the ultimately victorious Greeks. A statue of Leonidas stands still today at Thermopylae as a monument to stubborn courage.

OTHERS WHO FOUGHT TO THE DEATH

The Theban sacred band at Chaeronea, 338 BC

Jewish rebels at Masada, AD 73

Roman veterans resisting Boudicca at Colchester, AD 60

The Battle of the 300 champions, 545 BC

(In this last battle, Sparta and Argos decided to pit 300 champions against each other instead of fighting a conventional war. The final tally was 299 Spartans dead, to 298 Argives.)

COURAGE AS GRACE UNDER PRESSURE

We pour out a libation to Jupiter the Deliverer. Mark it well, young man, and may the gods avert the evil sign, but the times you have been born into mean that it is best you fortify your spirit.

THE STOIC THRAESA PATEUS IN DISCUSSION WITH HIS EXECUTIONER
AS HE WATCHES THE LIFEBLOOD FLOW FROM HIS VEINS.
TACITUS, *ANNALS*, 16.35

CLEOPATRA: SUICIDE IN STYLE

Centuries of Ptolemaic rule in Egypt came to an end with the death of Cleopatra VII, the last of her line. Cleopatra was both highly intelligent and charming, and had used her feminine wiles to ensnare first Julius Caesar, and then, even more spectacularly, Mark Antony. Sadly, Mark Antony was not the ideal choice of lover, since he was engaged in a massive struggle with Octavian, Caesar's adopted son.

When Octavian occupied Egypt, he had an interview with Cleopatra. Afterwards Cleopatra realized that the coldly brilliant Octavian had no interest in her other than as an ornament in his forthcoming triumph in Rome. This the proud queen of Egypt would not permit.

Though Octavian had her under close guard, she arranged for a snake – the highly poisonous asp – to be smuggled in with a basket of figs. 'Here it is,' remarked Cleopatra calmly, and held out her arm to be bitten. Because the queen had been cloistered with her maids for so long, a suspicious Octavian finally ordered the door broken down. He found Cleopatra dead, lying on a bed of cloth of gold, clad in her royal regalia. A maid, Charmion, had also taken poison, and was struggling to get Cleopatra's diadem right before she perished. 'Was this well done?' demanded Octavian angrily. 'It was exactly the right thing to do', replied Charmion with her dying breath, 'for she was the descendant of many kings.'

OVERACHIEVER, PART 2

Eutichtt, a woman of Tralles [in Asia Minor], who after she had given birth 30 times, was carried to her cremation by 20 of her children ...

PLINY THE ELDER, *NATURAL HISTORY*, 7.88

THE SUICIDE OF KING CLEOMENES I OF SPARTA

*Having got hold of a knife, he began to injure himself, starting from
the legs and working up. He went on cutting his flesh lengthways
from the legs to the thighs and from the thighs to the groin and sides,
until at last he came to the belly; and cutting this into strips, he died.*

HERODOTUS, *THE HISTORIES*, 6.74–5

OPTIONS FOR SUICIDES

Suicide in Greece and Rome generally took the following forms:

Stabbing oneself	**Seeking** death in battle
Opening one's veins	**Taking** poison
Starving to death	**Hanging** (this latter was considered unmanly and was generally left to women)
Suffocation (for example, by breathing charcoal fumes)	

In Greece and Rome, but particularly in Greece, suicide was seen as a form
of selfishness – a path only to be taken when there was no alternative.
Despite popular myth, a defeated Roman general was not expected to fall on
his sword, but rather to return home and face the consequences.

DECIMUS MUS: A LESSON IN SELF-SACRIFICE

In the early years, the Romans frequently found themselves with their
backs to the wall. One such occasion was in 312 BC, when a battle against
the combined Etruscans, Gauls and Samnites was not going well.

Decimus chose to do as his father had done a generation before.
After he had himself dedicated as a sacrifice to the gods of the underworld, he charged to his death among the enemy ranks. The sacrifice of
so eminent a general and consul both invigorated the Romans and
demoralized the enemy – both of whom knew that the sacrifice of the
previous Decimus Mus had led to a Roman victory. Once again, the
sacrifice was not in vain, and Roman arms triumphed handily.

THE DEATHBED

The delicate pyre was built with flammable papyrus,
The weeping wife was out buying cinnamon and myrrh,
There, with his grave, his bier
His undertaker all prepared,
Numa made me his heir –
And then got better.

MARTIAL, *EPIGRAMS*, 10.97

A BRIEF RETURN TO LIFE

*A. Viola, who had been Consul, came to his senses when
on his funeral pyre; but because the flames were so fierce
that he could not be rescued, he was burnt alive.*

PLINY THE ELDER, *NATURAL HISTORY*, 7.241

PLINY THE ELDER VERSUS MOUNT VESUVIUS

Pliny the Elder lived in the first century AD. He was a renowned scholar, some of whose researches have appeared in other parts of this volume. However, like many Romans of his day, he combined life as an academic with that of a man of action. As well as taking the time to research – for instance – the properties of minerals and the customs of faraway peoples, Pliny also was commander of the Roman fleet at Misenum, something that many thought constituted a full-time job by itself.

When in AD 79 his nephew (Pliny the Younger) pointed out to him a huge pillar of smoke coming from Vesuvius, Pliny's reaction to this huge natural disaster was not to flee but initially to get close to study it, and afterwards, when the scale of the disaster became apparent, to save as many people as possible.

Pliny remained calm throughout the disaster, even turning in for the night in a farmhouse and sleeping soundly while flaming pumice rained down on the roof. So dangerous were the falling stones that the group set off the next day with pillows strapped to their heads. They had not gone far when Pliny collapsed, overwhelmed by gaseous fumes from the volcano. He asked for a drink of water, and died soon after.

VERCINGETORIX: ACCEPTING DEFEAT

No one gave the Romans more trouble in the conquest of Gaul than the energetic and charismatic Gallic leader Vercingetorix. He caused the legions several setbacks before being cornered in the hilltop fortress of Alesia. When it became clear that the siege could not be broken, Vercingetorix surrendered to Caesar, knowing that the Romans would show no mercy.

Also the defenders of Alesia finally surrendered, though not before putting Caesar to no small trouble. The leader through the whole war was Vercingetorix. He put on his most beautiful armour and decorated his horse. Then he rode out through the gate. He circled Caesar, who remained seated, and then leapt from his horse. He then stripped off his armour, and sat at Caesar's feet. He did not move until he was taken away by those who would keep him imprisoned until the triumph. PLUTARCH, *LIFE OF CAESAR*, 28

At that triumph, Vercingetorix, as was traditional for a captured enemy leader, was killed by strangulation.

Vercingetorix in an idealized pose, from a statue erected in Gaul, which he was the first to unify into a nation.

LIFE OF A TYPICAL UPPER CLASS ATHENIAN MALE

Age 0–7 Remain at home in the women's quarters of the house

Age 7–18 Study under a tutor

Age 18 Become an ephebe (a junior citizen)

Age 18–20 Undergo ephebian training in military and civic affairs

Age 20 Become a fully signed-up Athenian

Age 30 (approx.) Get married, become eligible for most Athenian state offices

Age 40 Become eligible for all Athenian state offices

Age 50 No longer available for front-line military service

Age 60 Excused all military duties

Age 60+ Peaceful retirement and death

BLACK CLEITUS: A DISAGREEMENT AMONG FRIENDS

Alexander the Great was an epic drinker, and drunken quarrels were common in the Macedonian court, even when Alexander was on campaign. Incredibly, meetings to determine crucial strategies were often taken while the king and his advisors were well beyond tipsy.

On one such occasion, the king decided that a friend called Black Cleitus should leave the royal court and take up a position in Bactria (near modern Afghanistan). Cleitus did not want to go, and said so in no uncertain terms. It ended with a drunken shouting match in which Cleitus maintained that Alexander was no legitimate king of Macedon, and not half the man his father had been. While the guards studiously stayed neutral, an incensed Alexander hurled an apple at Cleitus' head while his friends hustled him out of the tent.

But Cleitus, who had probably thought of a juicy parting shot, barged back in only to run into a parting shot of Alexander's own – namely a javelin that the king threw into Cleitus' chest. Once sober, the king was remorseful, but at least Cleitus had his way – since he was dead someone else had to go to Bactria.

(Although fatalities were rare, such alcohol-fuelled free and frank exchanges were not. Indeed many years before, after just such a shouting match, Philip II had leapt from his couch at Alexander with murder in mind. However, he was so drunk that he fell flat on his face, allowing Alexander to escape and remark bitterly: 'My father, who plans to leap from Europe into Asia, is incapable of springing from couch to couch.')

DYING HAPPY

In the third century BC the Greek stoic philosopher Chrysippus played a dirty trick on his donkey by giving it wine and then watching the tipsy animal try to eat figs. The joke was on Chrysippus, as he laughed so much he had a convulsion and died.

THE DIADOCHI – THE SUCCESSORS OF ALEXANDER

Alexander's generals were unable to divide his empire peacefully between them – the result was a huge and complex series of wars in which most of the protagonists came to a sticky end.

Philip III Arrhidaeus Executed by Olympias in 317 BC

Perdiccas Assassinated by his soldiers in about 320 BC

Eumenes Executed by Antigonus in 316 BC

Antigonus I Monophthalmus Died in the Battle of Ipsus, 301 BC

Ptolemy I Lived to age 84, dying peacefully in 283 BC

Lysimachus Died in the Battle of Corupedium, 281 BC

Seleucus Assassinated by the son of Ptolemy in 281 BC

CATO THE YOUNGER – LIVE FREE OR DIE

In the last days of the Republic, the Roman Senate was a snakepit of political ambition and greed, dominated by immensely powerful and wealthy men. In this environment ('the sewer of Romulus', Cicero called it) one man could be relied on to do the correct thing. Not necessarily the best, most expedient, or most sensible thing, but the correct thing according to the strict principles of the early Republic.

He was in many ways the antithesis of the stylish, charming and utterly unprincipled Julius Caesar. Cato was prepared to die for the Roman Republic – Caesar was prepared to see the Roman Republic die for him. Unsurprisingly, the two men loathed each other. After his cause was defeated by Caesar in Rome's civil war, Cato chose death rather than to surrender and face Caesar's gloating forgiveness:

Cato drew his sword from its sheath and stabbed himself below the breast. His thrust, however, was somewhat feeble, owing to the inflammation in his hand, and so he did not at once dispatch himself, but in his death struggle fell from the couch and made a loud noise by overturning a geometrical abacus that stood near. His servants heard the noise and cried out, and his son at once ran in, together with his friends. They saw that he was smeared with blood, and that most of his bowels were protruding, but that he still had his eyes open and was alive; and they were terribly shocked. But the physician went to him and tried to replace his bowels, which remained uninjured, and to sew up the wound. Accordingly, when Cato recovered and became aware of this, he pushed the physician away, tore his bowels with his hands, rent the wound still more, and so died. PLUTARCH, *LIFE OF CATO*, 70

Cato's daughter, Porcia, was of a like mind. She actively encouraged her husband, Brutus, to assassinate Caesar. And when Brutus was later killed by the Caesarians, Porcia's friends kept close watch on her to prevent her imitating her father. But Porcia was set on suicide, and eventually managed this by scooping live coals from the fire and swallowing them.

LIFE EXPECTANCY IN GREECE AND ROME

Left *Vase painting showing an Athenian boy becoming an ephebe.*
Right *A fragment from an altar shows those most in danger of death – infants.*

At birth – 25 years

At age 10 – 41 years

At age 20 – 54 years

At age 30 – 59 years

At age 40 – 63 years

At age 50 – 67 years

At age 60 – 70 years

At age 70 – 76 years

It can be seen that in the ancient world, the longer you lived, the longer you were likely to live. Death happened mostly to the young – especially from illness in the first three years. If you were among the two per cent who lived to see 70 it meant that you had the dangers of either military service or childbearing years long behind you, and you were almost unkillable.

RECORD HOLDERS

M. Valerius Corvinus 100 years

Terentia, wife of Cicero 103 years

Xenophilus the Musician 105 years

Gorgias the Sicilian 108 years

Clodia, wife to Osilius 115 years

Galeria Copiola, a mime actress, first appeared on stage as a child in the consulship of Marius and last a century later, in plays dedicated to the health of Augustus, when she was 104

TARPEIA: ROCK STAR

One of the most infamous sites in Rome was named after Tarpeia, daughter of Spurius Tarpeius, commander of the Roman garrison on the Capitoline Hill during the earliest days of Rome. Tarpeia, it appeared, was very much a material girl, and she coveted the gold bracelets and armbands sported by Rome's enemies, the Sabines.

It did not take long for her to strike a deal. In the dead of night Tarpeia would allow the Sabines within Rome's defences. Since she was the daughter of the garrison commander she had access to the gates, and in return for letting the Sabines in, she demanded everything that each man carried on his arms. The 'everything' proved to be a mistake, as the Sabines also contributed the shields that they carried, heaping them one after another on the unfortunate traitor until she was crushed to death. Her body was then hurled from the heights of the Capitoline Hill.

This set a tradition in the Roman Republic by which those guilty of betraying Rome were not quietly strangled but taken to the heights of the 'Tarpeian Rock', and from there propelled living into the air to crash down to the edge of the Forum, ending up both mangled and dead. Thus the name of Tarpeia achieved a sort of gruesome immortality, but from the little we know of her character, she may well have been pleased with it.

AN UNKNOWN OPPONENT OF THEAGENES OF THASOS

Theagenes was a world-class competitor in the *pankration*, a particularly brutal boxing/wrestling event that he won in the Olympics of 476 BC. After his death, the citizens of his home town immortalized their sporting hero with a bronze statue.

A local rival of Theagenes, who had never won a bout against the great man, took his revenge by going every night to beat up the statue. However, even dead, Theagenes was an opponent to be feared, for after many nights of abuse the statue came loose from its base and toppled onto the frustrated rival, crushing him to death.

Theagenes, or rather his statue, was tried for murder (this being the way the Greeks did things) and on being found guilty of extreme unsportsmanlike conduct, the statue was dropped into the sea.

Greek boxer wearing nothing but the leather strips around his fists.

OTHO'S FAREWELL SPEECH

A debauched courtier of the emperor Nero, Otho surprised everyone by ruling with moderation, and, when his soldiers were defeated at Cremona, he decided that civil war was too great a price to pay for his continued grip on power. Tacitus records his farewell speech:

This courage of yours must not be put at risk again. I believe that too high a price to pay for my life. ... We have each taken the measure of one other, Fortune and I. Now you must not judge my reign by its duration, because it is harder for a man to be moderate in success when he thinks he will not enjoy it for long. ... Let this be the act by which posterity judges Otho. I require neither vengeance nor consolation. It may well be that others have been on the throne longer, but I shall make sure that no one leaves it more bravely. I cannot allow all these young Romans, all these fine armies, to be destroyed needlessly once more, and the country so harmed. TACITUS, *ANNALS*, 5.46

That night Otho retired to his tent with two daggers. He was found dead by morning, with a single stab wound in his chest.

LIFE OF A TYPICAL UPPER-CLASS ROMAN FEMALE

Age 5 (approx.) Start education

Age 6 Get engaged

Age 14 Officially leave childhood

Age 15–17 Get married

Age 21–30 Get divorced and remarried (many Roman women had serial marriages)

Age 40 (approx.) Become a widow (Roman husbands were typically 15–20 years older than their wives)

Age 40+ Amuse oneself by teasing those hunting for a legacy in your will

Roman matron.

DEATH IN SANCTUARY

DEMOSTHENES: HE WHO LIVES BY THE PEN DIES BY THE PEN

The Athenian orator Demosthenes led his city's resistance to the encroaching power of Macedonia. His speeches against King Philip of Macedon were inspirational calls to resistance. Indeed, it was written on his tomb that if Greece were as strong as Demosthenes was gifted, Macedon would never have won. However, the Greece of the third century BC was no match for the conquering power of Macedonia, and Athens fell under the sway of the invader.

When Alexander the Great died, Athens rose in rebellion, with Demosthenes among its leaders. The failure of the Greek cause meant that Demosthenes was doomed. The headhunters eventually tracked Demosthenes to the Temple of Neptune in Calauria (modern Poros), where he had taken sanctuary. Demosthenes agreed to leave the shelter of the temple once he had written a farewell to his family. After biting the end of his pen, as was his habit when composing, Demosthenes covered his head with his robe and became very still. The soldiers guarding the temple mocked his stillness, believing that the orator was paralyzed by fear. In fact Demosthenes was fast expiring from the poison that he had stashed in the hollow top of his pen against just this eventuality, preferring to die by his own hand than be slain by the enemy.

PAUSANIAS: DYING UNHARMED

The leader of the Greek armies that threw back the Persian invasion of Greece in the 490s BC was a Spartan. After his victory the ephors (Spartan magistrates charged with watching over their kings) reported that Pausanias was showing signs of letting his victory go to his head. As his rule became ever more despotic and erratic, the Spartans decided it was time for regime change.

Pausanias fled to the nearest temple, fully aware that the strictly religious Spartans would never violate the sanctuary of the temple by dragging him out. However, Spartan ingenuity was equal to the challenge, and they set about bricking up every door and window to the building. The mother of Pausanias was there with brick and trowel, declaring that it was better that her son should perish than become a threat to the state. When it was evident that their ex-king was on the verge of dying from hunger and thirst, the door was carefully unbricked, and Pausanias was taken outside to breathe his last. (This was less out of consideration for Pausanias than the fear of desecrating the temple by death.)

Stilicho: Last Orders, Please

Stilicho.

Stilicho was Rome's last great general. But trust was a rare commodity in AD 408, during the dying days of the western Roman empire, and the emperor Honorius believed that Stilicho was planning to replace him with his own son. Stilicho could easily have used his popularity with the army to lead a civil war that he had a good chance of winning. However, he correctly believed that Rome's last armies were too precious to be squandered in fighting each other.

Instead, Stilicho took sanctuary in a church, hoping that with the passing of time the emperor would come to his senses. And this is what appeared to happen. A group of soldiers appeared in front of the church, and an officer showed Stilicho his orders that if the general were to leave his sanctuary he would be conducted unharmed to the imperial presence. Trustingly, Stilicho left the church, whereupon the soldiers seized him. The officer then presented him with a later set of orders countermanding the earlier ones and ordering Stilicho's immediate execution.

Epitaph

Animula vagula blandula
hospes comesque corporis
quae nunc abibis in loca
pallidula rigida nudula
nec ut soles dabis iocos

Little soul, friendly and fleeting,
Guest and companion of my body
Where now do you go,
Pale, rigid and bare?
No longer playful,
As once you were.

EMPEROR HADRIAN, DIED AD 138

IMPERIAL ROLL-CALL

On average, over about 500 years, the Roman empire lost an emperor every six years. There was sometimes more than one emperor around at a time, but few (in fact, only one) gave up the post willingly.

Here are the prospects facing a Roman emperor as he ascends to the imperial throne (being a gladiator is marginally safer):

- Probability of being killed by your own soldiers: 24%
- Odds that you will be deposed or resign: 12%
- Chances of death through illness: 11%
- Odds of dying from old age: 10%
- Likelihood of assassination by family or courtiers: 8%
- Possibility of dying in battle: 8%
- Chances of being executed (e.g., by a usurper): 8%
- Likelihood of suicide to escape something worse: 7%
- Possibility of 'accidental' death: 5%

Individual departures from the most dangerous job in the ancient world are described on the following pages.

Above *Coin of Galba.*
Right *Bust of Trajan.*

(P) died peacefully; (V) violent death; (O) other death; (?) disputed or uncertain

THE JULIO-CLAUDIANS

Apart from Augustus, all died (or probably died) violent deaths.
This is less sad than it might appear, because by and large, the
Julio-Claudians weren't very nice people.

1 (P) AD 14 Augustus died of old age

2 (V) AD 37 Tiberius was probably suffocated

3 (V) AD 41 Caligula was assassinated by his guards

4 (V) AD 54 Claudius was poisoned by mushrooms

5 (V) AD 68 Nero committed suicide

THE YEAR OF THE FOUR EMPERORS

Only the last one, Vespasian, lived to see December.

6 (V) AD 69 Galba was killed by his soldiers

7 (V) AD 69 Otho committed suicide

8 (V) AD 69 Vitellius was killed by Vespasian's men

THE FLAVIANS

Although the Flavians were initially popular, it all ended in tears.

9 (P) AD 79 Vespasian died of old age

10 (O) AD 81 Titus died of a possible brain tumour

11 (V) AD 96 Domitian was assassinated

THE GOLDEN YEARS

The age of the Antonines, when emperors selected their successors,
had long reigns and expected to die in bed.

12 (P)(O) AD 98 Nerva, died of age and stress

13 (O) AD 117 Trajan died of a stroke

14 (O) AD 138 Hadrian succumbed to a heart condition

15 (P) AD 161 Antoninus Pius died of old age

16 (O) AD 169 Lucius Verus, co-emperor of Rome, died of the plague or
from a stroke

17 (P) AD 180 Marcus Aurelius died of old age

*Septimius Severus, one
of the fortunate ones.*

THE YEARS OF CRISIS

In the following 100 years being
emperor becomes *really* dangerous,
and only one (of 30) will die in bed.

18 Ⓥ AD 192 Commodus was assassinated

19 Ⓥ AD 193 Pertinax was killed by his soldiers

20 Ⓥ AD 193 Didius Julianus was executed by Septimius Severus

21 Ⓟ AD 211 Septimius Severus died of old age

22 Ⓥ AD 211 Geta was killed by his brother Caracalla

23 Ⓥ AD 217 Caracalla was assassinated

24 Ⓥ AD 218 Macrinus was executed

25 Ⓥ AD 222 Elagabalus was killed by his soldiers

26 Ⓥ AD 235 Alexander Severus was killed by his soldiers

27 Ⓥ AD 238 Maximinus Thrax was killed by his soldiers

28 & 29 Ⓥ and Ⓥ AD 238 Gordians I and II, father-and-son emperor team.
Son is killed in action, father hangs himself

30 & 31 Ⓥ and Ⓥ AD 238 Pupienus and Balbinus co-emperors killed by
soldiers

32 Ⓥ AD 244 Gordian III was killed by his soldiers

33 Ⓥ AD 249 Philip the Arab died in battle

34 Ⓥ AD 251 Decius died in action

35 Ⓥ AD 253 Trebonius Gallus killed by his soldiers

36 Ⓥ AD 253 Aemilius Aemilianus was killed by his soldiers

37 Ⓞ AD 260 Valerian died in captivity

38 Ⓥ AD 268 Gallienus was killed by his soldiers

THE EMPIRE OF THE GAULS

Since the Roman empire appeared to be going to pot, the western part virtually seceded and for 14 years was ruled by its own emperors. The empire was smaller, but the job was no safer.

39 Ⓥ AD 269 Postumus was killed by his soldiers

40 Ⓥ AD 269 Marius was strangled in a private quarrel

41 Ⓥ AD 271 Victorinus was killed by his soldiers

42 Ⓟ AD 274 Tetricus died of old age

THE MILITARY EMPERORS

Strong men, mainly from the Balkans, stabilized a failing empire and made life safer for its citizens. However, things remained highly risky for them personally.

43 Ⓞ AD 270 Claudius II died of the plague

44 Ⓥ AD 270 Quintillus killed himself

45 Ⓥ AD 275 Aurelian was killed by his soldiers

46 Ⓥ AD 276 Tacitus was murdered

47 Ⓥ AD 276 Florianus was killed by his soldiers

48 Ⓥ AD 282 Probus was killed by his soldiers

49 Ⓞ AD 283 Carus was hit by a thunderbolt

50 Ⓥ AD 284 Numerian was murdered

51 Ⓥ AD 285 Carinus was killed by his soldiers

52 Ⓟ AD 305 Diocletian died of old age

THE AGE OF CONSTANTINE THE GREAT

We now find an ever-increasing number of emperors resigning their post. This means they did not die on the job, but were generally assassinated soon afterwards, which does not represent a great improvement at the personal level.

53 Ⓥ AD 305 Maximian died by murder or suicide

54 Ⓟ AD 306 Constantius died of old age

55 Ⓥ AD 307 Severus II abdicated and was murdered

56 Ⓞ AD 311 Galerius, co-emperor, died of illness

57 (V) AD 312 Maxentius drowned

58 (V) AD 313 Maximinus committed suicide

59 (V) AD 324 Licinius abdicated and was murdered

60 (P) AD 337 Constantine 'the Great' died of old age

EASTERN AND WESTERN EMPERORS

The Roman empire had now two sets of emperors, which meant that as well as murderous family and subordinates, each emperor had also a potentially murderous counterpart.

61 (V) AD 340 Constantine II was killed in battle

62 (V) AD 350 Constans was killed by his soldiers

63 (O) AD 361 Constantius II died of illness

64 (V) AD 363 Julian the Apostate died in battle

65 (O) AD 364 Jovian died of carbon monoxide poisoning

66 (O) AD 375 Valentinian I died of apoplexy

67 (V) AD 383 Gratian killed by rebels

68 (V) AD 378 Valens died after defeat in battle

THE RULE OF THE PATRICIANS

Rome's last field army died with Valens, and thereafter the western empire was at the mercy of the barbarian hordes. Some 'barbarians' were co-opted into the defence of the empire, and eventually ended up running it, with the emperors as increasingly dispensable figureheads.

69 (V) AD 392 Valentinian II killed in a coup

70 (P) AD 395 Theodosius I died of old age

71 (?) AD 408 Arcadius died of unknown causes

72 (O) AD 423 Honorius died of illness

73 (V) AD 425 Johannes was executed

74 (O) AD 450 Theodosius II died in a riding accident

75 (V) AD 455 Valentinian III was assassinated

76 (V) AD 455 Petronius Maximus killed by barbarians

RICIMER'S EMPERORS

The German warlord Ricimer was for many years the true ruler of the west, making and unmaking emperors as it suited him.

77 Ⓞ AD 456 Avitus demoted

78 Ⓥ AD 461 Majorian deposed and executed

79 Ⓞ AD 465 Severus III deposed

80 Ⓥ AD 472 Anthemius executed

81 ⓘ AD 472 Olybrius died probably of plague

THE LAST WESTERN EMPERORS

In the final years nothing reflected the sad state of the Roman empire in the west better than the fact that the final heirs of Augustus were not considered worth killing.

82 Ⓞ AD 474 Leo I died of dysentery

83 Ⓞ AD 474 Glycerius was deposed

84 Ⓞ AD 475 Julius Nepos overthrown in a coup

85 Ⓞ AD 476 Romulus Augustulus retired

Imperial golden eagle.

THE GOLDEN EAGLE AWARDS

Shortest reign 44 (Quintillus). He lasted 17 days by some counts

Longest reign 74 (Theodosius II). He lasted 42 years

First runner up 1 (Augustus). Ruled for over 35 years

Youngest emperor 69 (Valentinian II). He became emperor at four years old

First emperor succeeded by a (non-adopted) son 9 (Vespasian)

Last pagan emperor 64 Julian the Apostate

ULTIMI VERBI IMPERATORUM
(*IMPERIAL LAST WORDS*)

I've made a mess of it.

CLAUDIUS, SUFFERING FROM FLATULENCE AS HE TRIES TO DIE WITH DIGNITY

———•◆•———

What an artist dies with me!

NERO, WHILE STABBING HIMSELF IN THE NECK

———•◆•———

What are you doing comrades? I am yours, and you are mine.

GALBA TO THE SOLDIERS WHO KILLED HIM

———•◆•———

And yet I was your emperor.

VITELLIUS, WHEN TAUNTED BY A SOLDIER AFTER HIS OVERTHROW

———•◆•———

Equanimity.

ANTONINUS PIUS GIVES THE WATCHWORD TO HIS GUARDS THEN
QUIETLY PASSES AWAY

———•◆•———

Mother, help! I am being murdered!

GETA, STABBED IN HIS MOTHER'S ARMS BY HIS BROTHER

———•◆•———

CLOSING TIME

———•◆•———

Oi, little book! You've had enough
Here we are at parchment's end
Yet you still want to go on and get fatter.
Show a bit of restraint here –
(We might have done too much by finishing page one)
Our reader is getting tetchy and impatient
And even the publisher is saying
'Enough now, little book, you're full'.

MARTIAL, *EPIGRAMS*, 4.89

ACKNOWLEDGMENTS

This book was even more of a team effort than usual, with dozens of friends and colleagues suggesting favourite anecdotes and memorable events. I'd particularly like to mention Adrian Goldsworthy and Ian Hughes for their military expertise, and Joanne Berry for providing some hard-to-locate material on Pompeii. Rachel 'Nephele' Peel of UNRV came through with invaluable source material at a critical moment, while Michael Whitby read the text from end-to-end and his thoughtful comments, suggestions and observations have made this an immeasurably better book. It goes without saying that any errors in the text are despite the efforts of those mentioned above, and the discredit for them belongs to me alone.

The younger Pliny has also been a great source of information as he passes on gossip, interesting stories and trivia to his friends, while the military miscellanea section owes much to Caesar (who never shied away from a good anecdote or two) and even more to Frontinus, who assembled a book of edifying stories about military matters. There's a collection of jokes in the appropriately named *Philogelos* (Laughter-lover) whose dim-witted protagonist I have called Elithio Phoitete. There is also Valerius Maximus and his short stories about famous men, and some of the more interesting digressions of Xenophon, Polybius and Cassius Dio. In short, given the thousands of pages of miscellanea already compiled in antiquity, the challenge was to decide what should be left out, rather than to seek material to put in.

All translations from ancient sources are my own or from the public domain, except for those on pp. 66 and 119, Artemidorus Daldianus, *Oneirocritica: The Interpretation of Dreams*, translated by Robert J. White (Original Books, Torrance, CA, 1990).

SOURCES OF ILLUSTRATIONS

INDEX